China and India: Opportunities and Threats for the Global Software Industry

CHANDOS
ASIAN STUDIES SERIES:
CONTEMPORARY ISSUES AND TRENDS

Series Editor: Professor Chris Rowley,
Cass Business School, City University, UK
(email: c.rowley@city.ac.uk)

Chandos Publishing is pleased to publish this major Series of books entitled *Asian Studies: Contemporary Issues and Trends*. The Series Editor is Professor Chris Rowley, Cass Business School, City University, UK.

Asia has clearly undergone some major transformations in recent years and books in the Series examine this transformation from a number of perspectives: economic, management, social, political and cultural. We seek authors from a broad range of areas and disciplinary interests: covering, for example, business/management, political science, social science, history, sociology, gender studies, ethnography, economics and international relations, etc.

Importantly, the Series examines both current developments and possible future trends. The Series is aimed at an international market of academics and professionals working in the area. The books have been specially commissioned from leading authors. The objective is to provide the reader with an authoritative view of current thinking.

New authors: we would be delighted to hear from you if you have an idea for a book. We are interested in both shorter, practically orientated publications (45,000+ words) and longer, theoretical monographs (75,000–100,000 words). Our books can be single, joint or multi-author volumes. If you have an idea for a book, please contact the publishers or Professor Chris Rowley, the Series Editor.

Dr Glyn Jones
Chandos Publishing (Oxford) Ltd
Email: gjones@chandospublishing.com
www.chandospublishing.com

Professor Chris Rowley
Cass Business School, City University
Email: c.rowley@city.ac.uk
www.cass.city.ac.uk/faculty/c.rowley

Chandos Publishing: is a privately owned and wholly independent publisher based in Oxford, UK. The aim of Chandos Publishing is to publish books of the highest possible standard: books that are both intellectually stimulating and innovative.

We are delighted and proud to count our authors from such well known international organisations as the Asian Institute of Technology, Tsinghua University, Kookmin University, Kobe University, Kyoto Sangyo University, London School of Economics, University of Oxford, Michigan State University, Getty Research Library, University of Texas at Austin, University of South Australia, University of Newcastle, Australia, University of Melbourne, ILO, Max-Planck Institute, Duke University and the leading law firm Clifford Chance.

A key feature of Chandos Publishing's activities is the service it offers its authors and customers. Chandos Publishing recognises that its authors are at the core of its publishing ethos, and authors are treated in a friendly, efficient and timely manner. Chandos Publishing's books are marketed on an international basis, via its range of overseas agents and representatives.

Professor Chris Rowley: Dr Rowley, BA, MA (Warwick), DPhil (Nuffield College, Oxford) is Subject Group leader and the inaugural Professor of Human Resource Management at Cass Business School, City University, London, UK. He is the founding Director of the new, multi-disciplinary and internationally networked *Centre for Research on Asian Management*, Editor of the leading journal *Asia Pacific Business Review* (www.tandf.co.uk/journals/titles/13602381.asp). He is well known and highly regarded in the area, with visiting appointments at leading Asian universities and top journal Editorial Boards in the US and UK. He has given a range of talks and lectures to universities and companies internationally with research and consultancy experience with unions, business and government and his previous employment includes varied work in both the public and private sectors. Professor Rowley researches in a range of areas, including international and comparative human resource management and Asia Pacific management and business. He has been awarded grants from the British Academy, an ESRC AIM International Study Fellowship and gained a 5-year RCUK Fellowship in Asian Business and Management. He acts as a reviewer for many funding bodies, as well as for numerous journals and publishers. Professor Rowley publishes very widely, including in leading US and UK journals, with over 100 articles, 80 book chapters and other contributions and 20 edited and sole authored books.

Bulk orders: some organisations buy a number of copies of our books. If you are interested in doing this, we would be pleased to discuss a discount. Please contact Hannah Grace-Williams on email info@chandospublishing.com or telephone number +44 (0) 1865 884447.

Textbook adoptions: inspection copies are available to lecturers considering adopting a Chandos Publishing book as a textbook. Please email Hannah Grace-Williams on email info@chandospublishing.com or telephone number +44 (0) 1865 884447.

China and India: Opportunities and Threats for the Global Software Industry

JOHN MCMANUS
MINGZHI LI
DEEPENDRA MOITRA

Chandos Publishing

Oxford · England

Chandos Publishing (Oxford) Limited
Chandos House
5 & 6 Steadys Lane
Stanton Harcourt
Oxford OX29 5RL
UK
Tel: +44 (0) 1865 884447 Fax: +44 (0) 1865 884448
Email: info@chandospublishing.com
www.chandospublishing.com

First published in Great Britain in 2007

ISBN:
978 1 84334 158 1
1 84334 158 1

© J. McManus, M. Li and D. Moitra, 2007

British Library Cataloguing-in-Publication Data.
A catalogue record for this book is available from the British Library.

Printed in the UK and USA.

John McManus dedicates this book to his mother and late father.

Mingzhi Li dedicates this book to his parents Li Yaohua and Hou Yuwen, and his wife Zhang Ying.

Deependra Moitra dedicates this book to his parents Dr Rathindra Kumar Moitra and Mrs Deepaly Moitra.

Contents

List of figures

List of tables

Acknowledgements

In preparing this book, we have drawn on various sources and, as usual, boldly exploited our friends and professional colleagues. We were fortunate to receive very useful advice and help from a great and distinguished set of people. We thank everyone for their invaluable help with our project. We are particularly grateful to:

Richard Heeks, University of Manchester
Neil Botten, University of Westminster, London
David Floyd, University of Lincoln
Parthasarathi Banerjee, NISTADS/CISR India
Erran Carmel, American University, Washington D.C.

John McManus would like to thank his academic colleagues in Corporate Strategy, University of Lincoln Business School, for their generous time and assistance and the contribution of ideas. He would also like to say a special thank you to Emeritus Professor Gerard de Zeeuw and Dr Don White for their special support and enthusiasm during the preparation of this text – the manuscript was written in parallel with the writing his PhD thesis.

Deependra Moitra would like to thank his wife, Dr Nandita Moitra, and daughter, Ilina Moitra, for their unconditional and enthusiastic support towards this project.

Finally, Mingzhi Li's work has been supported by China's National Natural Science Foundation (Project Numbers 70231010 and 70321001).

Preface

The penetration of software into all facets of life has been so significant that it is not an exaggeration to say that we live in a software-enabled world today. This has led to a flourishing, multi-billion dollar global software industry. However, over the last decade, several economic, demographic and technological factors have substantially impacted the global software industry landscape. Two very prominent developments have been the globalisation of software development, and the emergence of India, followed by China, as two major software nations. Although the development trajectory of the software industry in China has been different than that of India, both China and India are now competing for supremacy in the global software industry.

In recent times, both China and India have been variously described as 'emerging superpowers', 'transitioning economies to watch', and the like. Both countries are witnessing unprecedented inflow of foreign direct investment. Both China and India have achieved remarkable GDP growth rates in the last few years. And, while China's prominence on the global landscape can primarily be attributed to its manufacturing industry, India has emerged on the world map because of its superior software capability and a growing software services industry. Increasingly we are seeing a convergence, with China achieving a rapid growth in its software industry and India in the manufacturing sector. China and India have assumed such critical dimensions that these days every boardroom meeting invariably includes a discussion on China and India strategy.

Fascinated by their prominence on the global software industry landscape, this book is an attempt to present the structure and dynamics of the software industries in China and India. Our motivation stems from our curiosity to understand what implications China and India hold for the global software industry, and how they can strengthen their growing dominance. We present multi-level analyses and perspectives, seeking to paint a thorough picture of the software industries in China and India. In doing so, we discuss interrelationships between Chinese and Indian software industries, and discuss competitive strategies they can adopt for their growth. Much of what we present is based on our own industry experience and analyses. However, wherever suitable, we have drawn from published sources, all of which have been duly acknowledged.

We must note, however, that this book presents a 'time now analysis' of the Chinese and Indian software industries, which are rapidly evolving with changing competitive dynamics. The discussions, therefore, must be seen in that perspective. While China and India will undoubtedly be the two most significant players in the global software industry in the decades to come, who in the long run will leapfrog who to achieve global dominance remains to be seen.

We hope that the readers will find this book as interesting and insightful as much as we have enjoyed working on it.

John McManus
Mingzhi Li
Deependra Moitra

About the authors

John McManus PhD is Rushmore Professor in Management Sciences (USA) and Senior Research Fellow at the University of Lincoln (UK). He is the author of several business software and strategy related textbooks, including the widely acclaimed *Competitive Strategies for Service Organisations,* which he co-authored with Neil Botten. Prior to becoming an academic Dr McManus worked within the global software industry and is a recognised expert in software risk management. He can be contacted at: *jmcmanus@lincoln.ac.uk.*

Mingzhi Li is an Associate Professor of Economics at the School of Economics and Management, Tsinghua University, P. R. China. His major teaching and research interests are in the areas of microeconomic theory, industrial organisation, and electronic commerce. Mingzhi Li was awarded his PhD in Economics from the University of Texas at Austin in 1999. From 1990 to 1993, he worked as an economist at the State Information Center of China. He was awarded a Bachelor's degree in Mathematics from Nankai University in 1987 and a Master's degree in Operational Research from Shanghai Jiaotong University in 1990. Professor Li's research has led to publications on international journals including *Computational Economics, Information Economics and Policy, Information Technology and International Development, International Journal of IT Standards and Standardization Research* and *Electronic Commerce Research.* He can be contacted at: *limzh@em.tsinghua.edu.cn.*

Deependra Moitra is a senior corporate executive at one of the leading global IT consulting and services companies based in Bangalore, India, and has previously held senior managerial and technical positions with Lucent Technologies and Siemens. He specialises in global innovation management, and technology strategy and business innovation. He has advised multinational companies and venture capital firms, and serves on several advisory boards as well as journal editorial boards. A widely recognised expert on management of global innovation, Deependra is a frequent speaker at various forums around the globe and has several publications to his credit. He can be contacted at: *deependra@moitra .com.*

The global software industry

Introduction

For the last three decades, the United States of America (US) has maintained a dominant position within the global software industry at all levels, however, the increasing attractiveness and importance of the global software industry to developing economies such as China and India cannot be denied. Irrespective of country of origin, all firms have to start their business somewhere and it takes only a single company, as Microsoft proved, to jumpstart an entire industry.

Looking back in time, the global software industry began to grow significantly in the 1970s largely due to the efforts of IBM. As the software industry grew in economic importance, the industry became the subject of several investigations in the 1980s, all of them motivated by anxiety over individual competitiveness. For example, the (US) Department of Commerce report *A Competitive Assessment of the United States Software Industry in 1984* acknowledged the supremacy of the US in the international software industry and made a number of recommendations to ensure that the nation maintained its position. The recommendations primarily concerned improved intellectual property legislation, efforts to combat restrictive policy, and the elimination of tariff barriers against US software exports. No recommendations were made regarding the international competitiveness of the industry.

The US dominance of the software industry is attributed to its early advantages in research and development, and the investment made in emerging technologies. One of the hidden lessons from the many studies on international business is that investment does not happen by accident. Investment activities are organised and managed by firms and often by multinational firms. The multinational firm exists because it is able to carry out trade and investment at lower cost than its competitors and because it is able to exploit better the differential capabilities of nations (see Table 1.1).

Table 1.1	Top 10 multinational software firms by revenue per employee	
Rank 2005	Company	Software services revenue per employee ($)
368	Innovative Software Technologies	2,883,333
15	SYNNEX Corporation	1,985,796
129	iBasis Incorporated	1,220,833
29	Google Incorporated	1,054,663
23	CSK Corporation	751,049
109	ePlus	644,444
17	QUALCOMM Incorporated	642,105
2	Microsoft	595,050
227	LookSmart Limited	534,722
37	Adobe Systems Incorporated	530,426

Source: *Softwaremag.com*, The Software 500, 2005.

A perspective on growth

In broad terms three market classifications may be noted within the global software industry. These are: suppliers of professional services (e.g. EDS and Fujitsu), software products (e.g. Microsoft, Oracle and Sybase), and integrated systems (e.g. IBM and SAP). This broad structure has profoundly affected the shape of the software industry over the last 20 years. In terms of software sales Microsoft is the leading player. The information technology sector directly employs nine million people in high-wage, skilled jobs in more than 4,000 firms around the world. It also supports 21 million more professional information technology workers in a range of industries such as consultancy and systems integration. The information technology sector contributes over a trillion dollars a year to the global economy that includes: $420 billion from the information technology services sector, $330 billion from the hardware sector, $180 billion from packaged software sector[1] and a further $80 billion in software security and peripheral services (see Figure 1.1).

This rapid growth has created problems for the industry. The industry remains chronically short of skilled manpower. In Europe alone, it is

Figure 1.1 Global ICT sectors

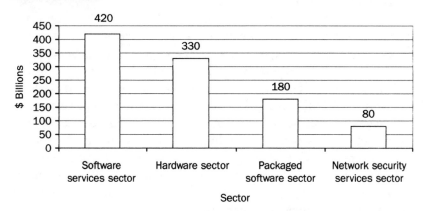

estimated that the industry is short of some 500,000 skilled workers. Japan and the US are also severely short of computer service personnel. This shortage continues to provide good opportunities for countries to take up this slack and provide skilled people to fill the gap. The international spread of the industry has not only resulted in the capturing of new markets, but also in providing opportunities to draw upon untapped pools of skilled workers. Although ninety per cent of the world's exports of software are from the US and Europe, evidence would also suggest that outside the US, UK, and Japan, the new and emerging countries within the software industry are China, India, and to a lesser extent Singapore and Malaysia[1].[2]

The emerging presence of China and India

The rise of both China and India as potential high-technology software competitors and important participants in the world's software industry has seemingly come as a big surprise to many foreign observers. The surprise is often accompanied either by overestimations or underestimations of the actual capabilities of these countries, rather like foreign reactions to the industrial success of Japan in the 1980s. While there are many important distinctions to be made between the Indian and Chinese cases, they are similar in that the development of software and technological capabilities in both countries has long been a goal of political, administrative, and industrial elites, and both countries have records of policy intent, planning, and making resource commitments for meeting that goal. This book examines some of their competitive strengths and weaknesses and the future market challenges faced by China and India in the next decade.

Although figures vary, these emerging markets currently account for around six per cent of global export markets. While 'lower cost' is the most commonly cited export reason, intense global competition in an environment of slower growth and low inflation demands constant vigilance over costs. Due to the low costs and high quality, using offshore resources in selected countries appears to have given the US an economic advantage. Beyond the cost incentive, global sourcing provides several other practical benefits, including the ability of multinational organisations to efficiently stage 24x7 operations, the opportunity to customise products and services to meet local needs, and the means of geographically deploying workers and facilities to succeed in globally dispersed, highly competitive markets.

A key driver in the US pursuit of foreign direct investment is cost savings; for example, Global Insight predicts that total savings from the use of offshoring are estimated to grow from $6.7 billion (this represents an assumed 40 per cent saving against what would have been spent if domestic resources had been used instead of offshore resource) to $20.9 billion between 2003 and 2008. In firms with annual turnovers in excess of $100 million dollars, the decision to use internal or external resources is determined by a mixture of both the hard dollar (quantitative) and the soft dollar (qualitative) costs.[3] Key reasons for perusing such arrangements include:

- the ability to leverage value from its IT operations and add dollars to the bottom line;
- the ability to gain access to technology, skills, and knowledge not internally available;
- the ability to improve business processes and enable organisational change;
- the ability to provide needed short-term services without adding to ongoing operational costs;
- the ability to focus internal IT resources on core strategic plans and projects.

In high-technology markets, significant benefits can be realised from prioritisation and determination of success criteria, as the firm is able to identify a complete and comparable set of costs and benefits regarding investment choices. For example, resource limitations, in-house skill sets and knowledge, and expected performance and outcome measures are important factors that must be analysed in making the decision to offshore. Establishing and analysing quantitative and qualitative criteria provides a bottom-line total that indicates which investment decision is most effective and states the reasoning used in reaching that decision. The use of offshoring is an efficient and effective alternative to using in-house resources, but a full determination of costs and benefits is required to make that decision. Successful decisions are dependent on having a clear understanding of all the options available.

Foreign direct investment (FDI)

FDI has increasingly been viewed as a catalyst to economic and market growth for those developing countries engaged in the computer software and services business, particularly in countries such as China and India (Table 1.2). More importantly, FDI as a principal conduit of transfer of technology, know-how and management skills, besides supplementing capital into developing countries, contributes to economic growth. The global competition for FDI among developing economies is increasing, with larger economies aiming for a higher share of the FDI pot. In this context, the two large emerging economies in Asia, wherein this competition is evident, are China and India. Both these economies are now getting increasingly integrated with the global economy as they open up their markets to international trade and investment inflows.

In developing its FDI strategies for the twenty-first century, the US is gradually moving away from the low-cost labour strategies of the past and is redirecting its resources to firms that have a focus towards leading-edge technology, research and development, high-quality infrastructure and clusters that can deliver value-added products and services. Here, Porter's concept of clusters attracting capital is pertinent; he defines a clustering model of firms working in a utilitarian manner where participants seeking to benefit from the cluster and contributing to it appeals to those firms with liberal business values.[4]

Although US firms have financially benefited from FDI, changes in how FDI is defined and used have led to conflicting information on how to make an effective decision about FDI; there seem to be conflicting opinions as to which models really represent value for money. For example, offshoring was used primarily to contract for data centre services and facilities management, as vendors provided economies of scale for mainframe use. In the 1980s, offshoring expanded to include

Table 1.2   Stages of growth in computer and software services for developing countries

Stage	Description of stage	Intellectual property rights (IPR) issues	Policy concerns
Level 1	Minimal computer software and services industry presence in country: what exists are a few sales/marketing outlets and some IT/software consultants	High level of piracy of computer software	Policy focused on improved consumption especially in terms of cost and access (of cheap/free software)
Level 2	Establishment of sales offices by major multinational computer and software service companies; possible local adaptation of major programmes by multinationals; very small nucleus of domestic companies focused around software local consultancy and adaptation work and overseas body shopping	High levels of piracy of computer software; initial concerns being raised by domestic software producers	Policy focus still on consumption but growing interest in developing a computer software and services industry (supply)
Level 3	More general inward investment by major computer service multinationals to access cheap but skilled labour; domestic software companies developing around the production of custom made software, outsourced coding work and continued body shopping	Clamp down on piracy to protect the industry begins mainly under pressure from overseas multinationals operating in the country	Twin policy focus on FDI and domestic computer software and services development. Policy shifts more strongly towards developing the industry (supply) as part of economic development

| Table 1.2 | Stages of growth in computer and software services for developing countries (Cont'd) |

Stage	Description of stage	Intellectual property rights (IPR) issues	Policy concerns
Level 4	Take-off of the domestically owned industry still focused on custom made software development; FDI by domestically-owned companies starts; continued build-up of overseas computer software and service; concern over increasing labour costs; growth in supporting institutional framework	Clamp down on piracy and acceptance of international intellectual property regimes that will protect the development of the domestic industry	Strong emphasis on computer software and services as sector for industrial policy
Level 5	Full international player status	Increasing attention toward global intellectual property right concerns	Global expansion but good domestic provision

Source: United Nations, UNCTAD, Geneva, 2002.

the goal of using only external resources and services to develop and manage all IT activities. As suggested above, the primary motivations were cost savings, the desire to avoid or defer high-risk capital investments in new technologies, and the need to focus on the core business processes of the organisation. Now, offshoring can refer to any of the above options, as well as to highly-defined contracts that 'out-source' relatively small chunks of service, and to managed services contracts in which an organisation monitors service provisions and alters their characteristics in real time. Offshoring individual business functions is now a more common activity than offshoring an organisation's entire IT infrastructure and management. Offshoring literature now places less importance on hard dollar cost savings and more importance on the business benefits, the soft dollar (or qualitative) savings, and the strategic purposes of offshoring selective pieces of the IT environment, such as research and development, application development and call centre services.

In formulating their offshoring policy and strategy, the US has gone to great lengths to protect its own self-interests: for example, employment law and investment decisions are predicated on the basis of governance and federal law, and whilst the US earns billions of dollars from its exporting activities there is strong opposition by labour groups and their political supporters to the offshoring of IT goods and services. Most of the IT jobs taken offshore have gone to China and India. Opposition within the US software industry has been fierce given that the US could lose up to 3.3 million jobs in the next 15 years, causing a loss of $136 billion in wages.

Global Insight has estimated that the number of US displaced IT software and services jobs due to IT offshoring as of 2003 was around 104,000. This includes not only jobs that were eliminated by some US companies that substituted offshore resources for domestic resources, but it also includes jobs that were never created, as other US companies expanded their IT activities using offshore resources without reducing their domestic resources. However, it is important to note that the total number of IT software and services jobs that have been lost since 2000 when the dot-com bubble burst is around 372,000 but only 2.8 per cent of the total IT software and services jobs were lost because of IT offshoring.

FDI and labour markets

A common worry for developing countries like China and India is FDI impact on domestic markets. As far as the labour market is concerned, the main question here is: does FDI export jobs? The question is complex, being not just related to job demolition, but also to job creation. In the category of job demolition, the negative effect on employment can result from a reduction in domestic output or it can originate from the existence of rigidities (poor mobility or excessive segmentation) in the labour market itself, which come into play when there is a shift in the composition of output. The first of the two cases emerges depending on when, in what way, and how far FDI and trade are substitutes. As was evident from the discussion about offshoring in the preceding section, there is no clear answer to this question. The second case is a more complicated one and it too does not have a unique answer. In fact, it requires that FDI and trade be complementary, and that the domestic sectors activated by the increase in the international production cannot react positively because of the presence of rigidities. Any mismatch can be expected in the future to either diminish, with the increase in education that should give more flexibility to China and India's labour markets, or to become even more acute, along with the increase in skill specialisation. We will briefly come back to the 'rigidity' (relative immobility of labour) later on in Chapters 4 and 5.

FDI and market growth

In the provision of software, two focal dimensions can be identified: market location (sales to export and/or domestic markets) and output type (sales of software products/or services). Both China and India have experienced substantial gross domestic product (GDP) growth rates of late. Growth in these countries has been led by a national strategy to promote their software industries generally and software exports in particular. The presence of a national software strategy for exports is therefore recognised as a vital part of software success. Critical to the success of each country has been a vision of what software could achieve for the country; a vision shared by a relatively small but committed group of government officials, CEOs and private entrepreneurs. Such visions first emerged in the 1970s, were sustained through the lean years in the 1980s, and only truly came to fruition in the 1990s. This has typically required institutional support within government, such as found in industry, for example India's National Association of Software and Services Companies.[5]

As part of this vision, attracting foreign investment has been one of the goals of both China and India. China for example, has benefited in 2002 from $ 52 billion of utilised FDI (Table 1.3).[6] For the host country, FDI brings many potential benefits. From the theoretical point of view, the benefits of FDI to China and India come from several different sources, all gathered together into two main categories: the transfer of technology and the externalities in the form of spillovers, that is, everything else that derives from FDI other than technology transfer or, in a slightly different and perhaps more precise view, productivity spillovers and market access spillovers.[7] In fact, the technology transfers in a proper sense cannot be other than direct, that is, transfers to the affiliates for intermediary, capital goods, or specialised equipment to be used by them, research and development, generated knowledge, instruction programs with visits and exchange of personnel. Nevertheless, once done, they must create spillovers to make the host country benefit from that, and it is commonly understood that the inflow of new technology and working practises from the affiliates creates a significant potential for spillovers to local firms in the host country. Still further productivity spillovers originate when:

1. A local firm improves its productivity by copying some technology used by multinational affiliates operating in the local market.

2. The entry of an affiliate leads to greater competition in the host economy, so that local firms are forced to use existing technology and resources more efficiently.

3. Competition forces local firms to search for new, more efficient technology.

If we leave aside the controversial aspect of causality between FDI and market or industrial concentration, the entrance of multinational enterprises to a market in the form of green-field investment doubtless increases competition in the short term. Increased competition in one sector could make local firms of this sector worse off, if they are not able to react positively, or better off, if they evolve and eventually adopt more efficient management and labour practices. At the same time the increased competition in that sector makes other sectors' firms better off through forward and backward linkages. Both aspects are beneficial: the former effect is likely to reduce prices for customer firms, the latter will generate a new demand for local production, thus increasing the pace at which competing products and processes of domestic origin appear in the local market, or helping develop proper local markets from the bottom where they do not yet exist.

FDI in China

In the last two decades, China has undertaken major restructuring and reform of its markets. FDI as stated above was one of the main pillars of reform. The Chinese government has gradually liberalised its restrictions on FDI in order to reap the rewards of foreign investment in technology transfer, modern management skills, and foreign exchange. The results of the reforms have been breathtaking. Thousands of multinationals firms have invested in China, bringing with them billions of dollars in FDI (Table 1.3).

As a member of the World Trade Organisation (WTO) since December 2001, China is revising its laws and regulations in order to allow further

Table 1.3   FDI in China (in millions of US dollars)

	2003	2004	2004 As a percentage of gross capital formation
Inward investment	53,505	60,630	8.2
Outward investment	−152	1805	−

Source: United Nations, UNCTAD World Investment Report 2005.

FDI and entice multinational firms to invest. It is also restructuring its centrally-planned economy to cater for the perceived influx of wealth. Many global software organisations have taken advantage of China's market reforms and investor confidence. Many software organisations that have expanded into China have taken advantage of its cost structure and 1.3 billion consumers to enhance profits and shareholder returns.

Although many companies have been successful, some have not achieved the gains they expected. Some of the newer entrants have done their research more thoroughly, however. For example, Motorola has captured one-third of the country's cellular phone market. The presence of multinational firms is without a doubt helping China to quickly become a leading producer of low- and high-technology products. The multinational firms that have entered China have brought an enormous amount of FDI. To date, $320 billion has been invested into the Chinese economy and China is today the third largest recipient of FDI in the world and the highest among the developing countries.

If China is to attract further inward investment, additional reform will be needed. In addition, the Chinese government recognises that entry into the WTO is the most effective way to encourage change and bring China into the global market place. After two decades of steady but halting reforms, Beijing is racing to dismantle the last vestiges of a command economy.[8] Although China has made significant progress in the past two decades, there is still a long way to go before their economy can be characterised as market driven and open. Therefore, the government is implementing another wave of reforms that will cement its membership of the WTO. These include:

- Inward investment in its telecommunications industry; permitting foreign equity share participation for value-added services (including e-mail, Internet and voice mail).

- Within five years of accession, allowing 49 per cent of foreign equity share for mobile and data services.
- Increased access in banking, insurance and securities.
- Increased access for professional services, including information technology, engineering and consultancy.
- Elimination of trade and foreign exchange balancing.
- Enforcement of intellectual property rights – specifically the trade-related aspects of intellectual property rights (TRIPS) agreement of 1996 (essential in combating piracy of US software and creating a healthy environment for China's software industry).

Article 7 of the TRIPS agreement is worth noting here. This article holds that the protection and enforcement of intellectual property rights should contribute to the promotion of technological innovation and to the transfer and dissemination of technology. This should be to the mutual advantage of producers and users of technological knowledge and in a manner conducive to social and economic welfare and to a balance of rights and obligations. Further changes to TRIPS are likely to occur that take into consideration issues raised by new technological and other developments. Many developing countries feel that TRIPS is not in their favour. When extending intellectual property rights, consideration should be given to other rights, such as access to information, freedom of expression and knowledge of social justice.[9]

The reforms that China has committed to in its agreement with the United States should strengthen the regulatory framework and open the country to increased foreign investment. Chinese decision makers have also turned their attention to standards as part of the strategy for meeting new competitive challenges and obligations resulting from China's accession to the WTO. Representatives from the international business community and officials of foreign governments have followed Chinese approaches to standardisation with growing interest as these not only effect business decisions, but also raise questions about the use of a policy tool to unfairly enhance the competitiveness of Chinese industry in ways that would be inconsistent with China's WTO commitments. Nevertheless, as China improves the transparency of its trade regime to meet the standards set by the WTO and gives more secured access to Chinese goods in the overseas market, more foreign investors are likely to seek export operations on the mainland. Opening up distributions will attract additional inflows from telecommunications and banking.

Future challenges

In spite of the opportunities available for attracting FDI, several challenges remain to be met in order for the economy to sustain an even higher rate of growth and enhanced competitiveness. China has gained some competitive advantage in technology-intensive goods, and has improved its capability in production and export of components. China currently has an advantage over the majority of its competitors in other developing countries due to its low wages (and its ability to add value at the margin). If China is to attract further FDI and preserve its competitive position, it will be absolutely crucial to maintain a low-cost strategy and build capacity (and capital reserves) in high-technology sectors.

The information, communications and technology markets have proven very lucrative for India, and China is now looking to attain comparative advantage in this area. However, responding to this reality requires skilful execution in a global economy where established standards already provide a framework for successful economic activities. Skilful execution of a technology strategy under conditions of globalisation will require steering between extremes of a narrow techno-nationalism likely to cause friction and resentment from trading partners and a possible marginalisation of China's industry, and a techno-globalism insensitive to national economic interests. The key, according to Atsushi Yamada, is a mixture of expanded state commitments and public private partnerships enthused with openness towards foreigners in national technology programs, and greater commitment to international rule making and policy coordination (see Chapter 8).

As previously alluded to, China's software sector is strongly linked to the domestic market due to its focus on product development; India's software industry has grown mainly through focusing on exports. Thus, capabilities amongst Chinese and Indian firms differ significantly in the software industry, which has important implications for the possible strategies that firms in both countries can undertake to develop and retain their comparative advantages. China's strategic adjustment into the worlds export markets will rely to some degree on its ability to replicate India's strong capabilities in process maturity and management skills.

FDI in India

India did not begin to liberalise its economy until a decade later than China. However, India's market-oriented economic reforms, undertaken in

1991, were directed towards increased liberalisation, privatisation and deregulation of the industrial sector, and to the re-orienting of the economy towards global competition by the reduction of trade barriers and gradual opening up of its capital account. This has increasingly led to India becoming a favourable destination for foreign investors.

With a consumer market of approximately 1.1 billion people, the increased globalisation of the Indian economy has opened up significant business opportunities for investors throughout the world. These opportunities are increasingly opening up for the services sector, whose share in the economy has been rising significantly. The Indian economy has been relatively successful in increasing its trade openness and attracting FDI inflows, and also in promoting the services sector as an engine of future growth (Table 1.4).

Even though India has been a latecomer to the FDI scene compared to east Asia, its significant market potential continues to attract foreign investors. However, several challenges remain to be met in order to sustain a higher growth path for the economy, and enhance competitiveness in order to position itself favourably in the global competition for FDI. India's share in world trade has shown a continuous and sharp increase in the last 10 years. This indicates India's greater integration with the world economy since 1991, the year when economic reforms to liberalise the economy were introduced. This growth has been accompanied by a significant improvement in the strength of the external sector, and in export performance, during the post-reform period. Growth of India's exports of goods and services has more than doubled since 1992, with its share in India's GDP increasing substantially.

Although China has benefited more from inward investment, India remains attractive as a destination for FDI with its increased liberalisation of trade and investment policy regime. There has been a progressive liberalisation of the capital account, which has contributed to an increased flow of two-way investments both in and out of India

Table 1.4   **FDI in India (in millions of US dollars)**

	2003	2004	2004 As a percentage of gross capital formation
Inward investment	4269	5335	3.4
Outward investment	913	2222	1.4

Source: United Nations, UNCTAD World Investment Report 2005.

(Table 1.4). Foreign ownership of up to 74 per cent of equity is now allowed in selected high-priority infrastructure sectors, ranging up to 100 per cent foreign ownership on an automatic basis for investment proposals in ports, roads and power generation. Indian companies are now allowed to invest in subsidiaries and joint ventures abroad, with individuals, companies, and mutual funds also being allowed to invest in overseas listed companies.[10] In the case of mutual funds, the limit has been raised to US$ 1 billion on mutual funds from the previous US $500 million. As a result, both equity and portfolio investment abroad have been considerably liberalised. In the process, India is now moving further towards capital account convertibility.

Compared to China, and in spite of a decade of reforms, India appears to remain an underperformer in the global competition for FDI. However, conclusions based solely on those figures in Tables 1.1 and 1.2 need to be interpreted carefully, as the above indexes have used FDI data provided by official sources in each country whose definition and measurement methods vary significantly. This is often not taken into account when making international comparisons of FDI data, which could influence investor perceptions.

FDI inflows in India began in earnest only after the 1991 reforms. These significantly liberalised FDI flows by creating a discretionary mechanism of approval through the Foreign Investment Promotion Board (FIPB) and an automatic approval mechanism, particularly for investment in infrastructure, through the Reserve Bank of India. The US has been the single largest investor in India, accounting for approximately a quarter of India's approved FDI during the 1991 to 1995 period. Thereafter, its share has been declining relative to other investor countries, namely the UK, Netherlands and France. Mauritius ranks as the second highest investor country, mainly due to FDI being routed through Mauritius as it has a double taxation treaty with India. India has been attracting higher volumes of FDI from US and Europe, compared to Asia.

Before the economic reform in the 1990s, FDI was heavily concentrated in manufacturing activities, which was due to import-substituting industrialisation that encouraged tariff-jumping investments to capture the protected domestic market.[11] The trend in recent years has changed towards an increase in foreign investment in the tertiary sector that encompasses mainly services activities. These include the information and communication technology (ICT) sector (comprising of telecommunications, computer software, consulting services, etc), as well as power generation, and hotels and tourism. The share of services sector (including all the above) in total FDI inflows rose significantly from 5 per cent in 1990 to 52 per cent during 1991 to 2001.

Future challenges

In spite of the opportunities available for attracting FDI in India, several challenges remain to be met in order for the economy to sustain a higher growth path, and enhance competitiveness in order to position itself favourably in the global competition for FDI.

The main challenge to sustaining globalisation in the Indian economy at the domestic level lies in the successful implementation and continuation of the second-generation reforms. These reforms are directed towards reducing structural impediments to higher growth and are designed to focus on fiscal consolidation, institutional reforms, poverty eradication, and provision of adequate social safety nets, infrastructure development, enhancing manufacturing sector efficiency and attracting growth enhancing investment in the country. Such wide-ranging reforms would enhance India's capacity to engage effectively in international competition, thereby providing greater opportunities to harness its growth potential. There is some evidence to suggest that the competition among states is intensifying and could act as a lever to utilise growth-oriented policies across the country.[12] It is, however, important to ensure that inter-state competition in attracting domestic investment and FDI is healthy and promotes all-round development of the economy a clear challenge for the Indian political class.

As stated earlier, India has built up a significant software and services industry and is increasingly investing its reserve capital in new start-ups. There is growing concern amongst India's CEOs that multinational firms may bring obsolete technology into the country and invest in low-technology consumer products, as they are interested mainly in short-term profits, increasingly not adding to the value of productive GDP. It therefore becomes important to minimise the potential drawbacks and maximise the benefits from FDI in the form of productivity gains and cost reductions in the production process through better management of resources, access to superior technology and improvement of the quality and variety of goods available in the market. Micro-level research, focused on selected sectors, needs to improve the quality of this debate in India.

After Japan, China is the largest economic power in Asia and represents a significant challenge for India. On the eve of China's accession to the WTO, its GDP per capita (US$ 909) was almost double that of India (US$ 487) during 2001, while its gross national income in purchasing power parity terms was also higher by the same magnitude than that of the Indian economy. If the Indian economy cannot position itself favourably to enhance its global competitiveness, this economic gap is likely to increase further.[13]

Conclusions

China's accession to the WTO provides an important challenge for India's global competitiveness. India's strategy should be to avail itself of the opportunities that are offered by China's domestic market. This would require a long-term economic investment strategy. One mechanism for Indian firms would be to partner Chinese firms in their domestic markets, particularly in software, wherein Indian firms have already established a comparative advantage. Such a partnership would be helpful for Indian firms to draw lessons from their Chinese counterparts, and improve upon their capabilities. This implies that apart from attracting inward FDI for development of domestic market capabilities, India would need to encourage further outward FDI as well, in order to compete more effectively in the global market.

Notes

1. IDC's Analysis on Worldwide Software Revenues, 2004.
2. Floyd, D. and McManus, J. (2005) 'The role and influence of foreign direct investment on the development process: the case of the software industry in Romania, China, India and Philippines', *Global Business and Economics Review*, 7.
3. Botten, N. and McManus, J. (1999) *Competitive Strategies for Service Firms*. Oxford: Macmillan.
4. Porter, M.E., Takeuchi, H. and Sakakibara, M. (2003) *Can Japan Compete?* Oxford, Macmillan. See also: Simon, D.F. (2003) Presentation made at the Conference on China's Emerging Technological Trajectory in the Twenty-first Century, Rensselaerville, NY, September 4–7.
5. Heeks, R. and Nicholson, B. (2002) *Software Export Success Factors and Strategies in Developing and Transitional Economies*. Manchester, UK: IDPM.
6. Western analysts anticipate a 10 per cent rise in utilised FDI in China in 2003. Source: USCBC.

7. Blomström, M. and Kokko, A. (1998) 'Multinational corporation and spillovers', *Journal of Economic Surveys*, 12(3): 247–77.
8. *Business Week*, April 16, 2001.
9. Queau, P. (2000) 'Who owns knowledge?', *Le Monde Diplomatique* (English Edition).
10. See *http://www.blonnet.com/2003/05/21/stories/2003052102640500.htm*
11. Munjal, P. and Pohit, S. (2001) *Perceptions of Impact of FDI on Economy*. Report prepared for the Centre for International Trade Economics and Environment (CUTS): Mimeo.
12. Shand, R. and Bhide, S. (2001) 'Growth in India's state economies before and with reforms: shares and determinants', paper presented at the ASARC conference on Ten Years of Economic Reforms in India. The Australian National University, November 19–20; p. 24.
13. Martin, W. and Ianchovichina, E. (2001) 'Implications of China's accession to the World Trade Organisation for China and the WTO', *The World Economy*, 24: 1205–19.

2

China: a PESTEL analysis

Introduction

When considering the issue of comparing India and China, the most simple language to describe the differences between the two countries is 'the world's largest democracy' versus 'the world's largest autocracy'.[1] Although this metaphor indeed reflects some truth, the reality is much more complex. Generally speaking, it is still very controversial with regard to whether democracy promotes or hinders economic development in a developing country: 'But it remains sadly true that the free market that has helped the tigers so much often works better in Communist China than in India – not least thanks to India's own democratically elected Communist politicians.'[2]

In order to understand the environments for the development of the two countries' software industries and markets, a comprehensive investigation of their political, economic, societal and technological systems is a must. A comparison of the business environments of China and India's software industries can help understand why and how they have embarked on such different paths, and whether there is a suggestion that their future paths will converge in the globalised world. This chapter will give a description of some of the macro level variables that have directly or indirectly determined the current status and the future of China's software industry development, and presents a PESTEL (political, economic, social, technological, environmental and legal) analysis of the Chinese software industry.

Since the economic reform era started in 1979, China has been experiencing an impressive transformation from a closed, planned economy into a gradually opening and market-oriented society. The pace of change has been unprecedented in the nation's long history, and it is also quite remarkable even put in the perspective of world history. In the past 25 years, the country has reduced the number of its citizens living in poverty by 200 million and achieved a sixfold increase in per capita income. China accounted for nearly 4 per cent of the worldwide gross domestic product in 2004, and has become the sixth-largest economy and a leading recipient of FDI. The two major driving forces of the economic and social development have been the foreign investment and the opening of the economy to the outside world. A distinct feature of the growth of FDI in China was the pivotal role played by overseas Chinese. Some 50 per cent of inward FDI originated from the ethnic Chinese economies of Hong Kong, Taiwan, and Macao as of 1998.[3]

After several decades of rapid economic development, China is now facing some new challenges in formulating a sustainable development strategy. One major weakness of the reform has been the uneven and fragmentary institutional change and that the entrepreneurial, managerial and technical skills required for developing globally competitive firms remain scarce.[4] As found by an OECD study, China's economy has reached a stage that calls for some important changes in the way economic reforms are carried out. The important engines that have driven China's growth in the past are losing their dynamism since China's economy has become badly fragmented and segmented, and this has led to increasing under- and inefficient utilisation of resources. The study highlights three objectives as the key to the success of China's overall reforms over the next decade:

1. The first and most immediate is to lay the foundations for improving the utilisation of resources, by removing present obstacles to business sector restructuring and by achieving better integration among various segments of the economy that have been developed separately under different sets of rules.

2. The second is to improve competition law, property rights, enterprise governance and other frameworks that are essential to efficient market functioning, so that resources are efficiently allocated in the future.

3. The third is to improve the capacity of the government to support economic development, by strengthening the effectiveness of macroeconomic policies while refocusing the role of regulatory policy on establishing and enforcing rules for market behaviour.[5]

All three aspects will have some important implications for China's software industry development that we will explore in more details in Chapter 4, on the SWOT analysis of China's software industry.

One milestone in China's economic development has been access to the WTO, which has put China's economy on an irreversible trajectory. At the end of this chapter we will discuss the impact of China's WTO accession on its information technology industry and the software sector in particular.

Overview of China's software industry

In the era of planned economy, the software industry barely existed in China. The government devoted most of its financial resources and limited pool of skilled labour to reverse engineering key hardware, such as integrated circuits and technologies, with mixed military and civilian importance. There were scattered software development projects in state-owned research institutes, but commercial research and development was largely non-existent because of the organisational and institutional barriers separating these research institutes from the market. In some sense, the genesis of China's software industry can be traced back to the early 1980s with the creation of some spin-offs from government research institutes such as the Academy of Science.[6]

Software has been the weakest sector in China's ICT industry. Among all the reasons, the relatively favourable investment policy towards hardware could be an important factor. From 1993 to 2001, the major share of China's ICT investment went to the telecommunications industry, with the information consultation and computer service industry (software industry included) receiving a very small proportion (Table 2.1 and Figure 2.1).

However, signs that the software industry is slowly picking up have already been seen, with its contribution to the ICT industry increasingly steadily. In the past 10 years, China's software industry revenue has been growing at an annual rate of between 20 to 40 per cent, and in the last three years software exports have almost doubled every year (Table 2.2).

Table 2.1   Investment in ICT

100 million Yuan	Telecoms	Electronic and communication equipment manufacturing	Information consultation	Computer service
1993	218.82	47.49	0.14	0.16
1994	409.04	47.39	0.17	0.09
1995	491.94	65.84	0.6	0.12
1996	594.09	67.34	0.22	0.14
1997	343.56	122.4	2.27	0.8
1998	477.86	178.05	3.72	2.09
1999	469.42	146.01	3.36	8.22
2000	679.04	214.8	3.36	25.44
2001	769.93	298.57	13.3	34.86

Source: Compiled from the China Statistics Yearbook (1993–2002); China Statistics Press.

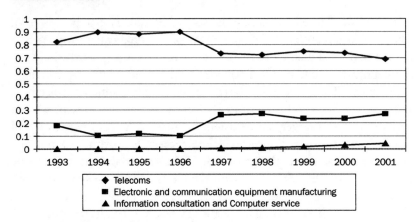

Figure 2.1 Shares of ICT investment

- ◆ Telecoms
- ■ Electronic and communication equipment manufacturing
- ▲ Information consultation and Computer service

China's software industry is capable of providing diversified software products, including platform software, middleware software, and application software. The application software, including enterprise resource planning (ERP) and accounting software, accounts for a larger

Table 2.2 The growth of the software industry in China (1990–2001)

Year	The total revenue of software services (billion RMB)	The total revenue of software products (billion RMB)	Annual growth rate of software products (%)	Exports of software (billion RMB)
1990	–	0.22	–	–
1991	–	0.46	100	–
1992	2.3	1.98	335	–
1993	4.9	4.0	100	–
1994	5.8	4.9	22.5	–
1995	7.7	6.8	38.8	–
1996	11.3	9.2	35.5	–
1997	14.8	11.2	21.7	–
1998	18.7	13.8	23.2	–
1999	23.8	17.6	27.5	2.1
2000	32.2	23.8	35.2	3.3
2001	40.6	33.0	38.7	6.0

Source: compiled from the Bulletin of China Software Industry Association (2001; http://www.csia.org.cn), CCID (2001; http://www.computerworld.com) and Computer World (2000; http://www.ccidnet.com).

share than other types. Table 2.3 shows that China has a huge domestic market for application software. In 2002, application software accounted for 64.5 per cent of the total domestic software products made in China.

Up to 2002, China had over 10,000 enterprises and 600,000 people engaged in the software and software services industry. By 2002, China also had 1,023 higher education institutions that offered computer and software programs, recruiting a total of 586,000 students. The Ministry of Education and the State Development Planning Commission have also established 35 software colleges to train and develop a skilled base of software programmers.

China's software industry: a PESTEL analysis[7]

China's political environment

One of the most important characteristics of China's political environment is the unchallengeable one party rule, which has been written into China's constitution. The Chinese Communist Party (CCP)

Table 2.3 The structure of software products in China (1992–2001)

Year	System software		Maintenance software		Application software	
	Revenue RMB 10 million	Proportion (%)	Revenue RMB 10 million	Proportion (%)	Revenue RMB 10 million	Proportion (%)
1992	1.6	8	5.4	27	12.8	65
1993	3.6	9	10.8	27	25.6	64
1994	4.5	9	13.2	27	31.3	64
1995	6.5	10	15.0	22	46.5	68
1996	8.5	9	20.0	22	63.5	67
1997	13.7	12	27.5	25	70.8	63
1998	17.4	13	35.9	26	84.7	61
1999	21.0	12	44.8	25	110.2	63
2000	33.2	14	49.6	21	155.0	65
2001	50.0	15	81.9	25	198.1	60

Source: compiled from the Bulletin of China Software Industry Association (2001; http://www.csia.org.cn), CCID (2001; http://www.computerworld.com) and Computer World (2000; http://www.ccidnet.com).

has governed China since 1949. Deng Xiaoping, who led the party – and therefore China – from 1978 to 1997, began a policy of 'socialism with Chinese characteristics', encouraging more economic openness and foreign trade.

Theoretically, the party's highest body is the Party Congress, which is supposed to meet at least once every five years. The primary organs of power in the Communist Party include:

- The Politburo Standing Committee, which currently consists of nine members;
- The Politburo, consisting of 24 full members, including the members of the Politburo Standing Committee;
- The Secretariat, the principal administrative mechanism of the CCP, headed by the General Secretary;
- The Central Military Commission;
- The Discipline Inspection Commission, which is charged with rooting out corruption and malfeasance among party cadres.

The Chinese government has always been subordinate to the Chinese Communist Party; its role is to implement party policies. The primary organs of state power are the National People's Congress (NPC), the President (the head of state), and the State Council. Members of the State Council include the Premier (the head of government), a variable number of vice premiers (currently four), five state councillors (protocol equivalents of vice premiers, but with narrower portfolios), 22 ministers and four State Council commission directors.

Under the Chinese constitution, the NPC is the highest organ of state power in China. It meets annually for approximately two weeks to review and approve major new policy directions, laws, the budget, and major personnel changes. These initiatives are presented to the NPC for consideration by the State Council after previous endorsement by the Communist Party's Central Committee. Although the NPC generally approves State Council policy and personnel recommendations, various NPC committees hold active debate in closed sessions, and changes may be made to accommodate alternate views. When the NPC is not in session, its permanent organ, the Standing Committee, exercises state power.

Despite the growing interest in political liberalisation, the central government had little intention of reducing its authority and was cautious about inciting increased political pressure. After the disastrous period of the Great Cultural Revolution, which came about under the excuse of giving the common Chinese people more freedom to fight against government bureaucracy, Chinese leaders since Deng Xiaoping have realised the importance of a political and social environment in which economic prosperity can develop. On the positive side, China is experimenting with free elections at the village level and is expected to broaden the scope of these up to the township and even country levels, but the pace of this widening remains to be seen. The government's direct interference in China's economy is unparalleled in the world. The power of the party can speed up the decision-making process, but can also cause inefficiency and wasting of resources as the power can be easily abused.

Reducing corruption and other economic crimes will be a critical issue in China's further economic and political reform.

China's economic development[8]

China's economy during the last quarter of a century has changed from a centrally-planned system that was largely closed to international trade to a more market-oriented economy that has a rapidly-growing private sector and is a major player in the global economy. Reforms started in the late 1970s with the phasing out of collectivised agriculture, and expanded to include the gradual liberalisation of prices, fiscal decentralisation, increased autonomy for state enterprises, the foundation of a diversified banking system, the development of stock markets, the rapid growth of the non-state sector, and the opening of the country to foreign trade and investment. The restructuring of the economy and resulting efficiency gains have contributed to a more than tenfold increase in GDP since 1978. Measured on a purchasing power parity (PPP) basis, in 2005 China stood as the second-largest economy in the world after the US, although in per capita terms the country is still lower middle-income and 150 million Chinese fall below international poverty lines. Economic development has generally been more rapid in coastal provinces than in the interior, and there are large disparities in per capita income between regions. Foreign investment remains a strong element in China's remarkable expansion in world trade and has been an important factor in the growth of urban jobs.

In a marked difference from the 'big bang' approach of economic reform as implemented in the former Soviet Union block, China has generally implemented reforms in a gradual or piecemeal fashion. China's economic reform in the past has demonstrated a tendency toward experimentation, making incremental changes to test reforms before implementing them on a national basis. While this did not lead to the success of all reform programs, it did help minimise risk, reduce the number of failed initiatives, and create momentum for the widespread adoption of change. By contrast, this approach meant that policy changes were 'not carried out according to comprehensive blueprint, but rather [were] piecemeal and ad hoc, best summarised by the Chinese phrase "crossing the river by feeling the stones"'. Given the complexity and interdependence of China's challenges, some argued that a more cohesive reform strategy was needed. Past policies to develop individual segments of the economy were based in part on the limited development of markets and their supporting mechanisms in the early stages of the reform era. As the scope for market forces has progressively increased and development has advanced, the administrative distinctions among these segments have come to have less and less economic meaning. Problems in individual areas and the policies needed to deal with them have become increasingly interdependent.

The economic transition has created great pressure on employment. The government has struggled to sustain adequate jobs growth for tens of millions of workers laid off from state-owned enterprises, migrants, and new entrants to the work force; from 100 to 150 million surplus rural workers are adrift between the villages and the cities, many subsisting through part-time, low-paying jobs. As the most populous nation in the world, China needs to create 100 million new jobs by 2013 and quadruple its GDP by 2020 to achieve and sustain a reasonable standard of living for its people.

On 21 July 2005, China revalued its currency by 2.1 per cent against the US dollar and moved to an exchange rate system that references a basket of currencies. Recently there have been signs of a clear trend that China is speeding up reform in the banking sector and the capital market in order to follow international standards.

China's society

China's society is operated on relationships, or 'Guanxi', which has been identified by academics and the business world as the most important characteristic of the Chinese society for an outsider to understand. Despite the fact that concurrent with the rapid economic growth and the influence of the western culture, a dramatic transformation of the Chinese society has been going on, building up 'Guanxi' will be important for firms to succeed in China's markets. Kai-Fu Lee, the ex-Microsoft executive hired by Google to head its Chinese operations, has studied the successful experiences of such multinational firms as Intel, Motorola and Samsung, and made the following observation about China's society: 'China's culture is built on trust, relationships, and mutual respect. Trust takes a long time to build, but there are many ways to break trust: by showing disrespect, by failing to provide favours in exchange for favours received, by not following the protocols, by condescending, coercion, or by dwelling on controversial issues. Trust is built on fulfilled promises. Ideally, the best scenario is to make promises and fulfil them. Keep in mind that it is much better to not make promises than to over-commit and fall short.'[9]

The importance of building Guanxi has very significant implications for software firms in conducting business. The problem caused by the Guanxi-based business connection is the unpredictability of the business environment. The identification and promotion of select producers, by providing government contracts, potential access to capital, and regulatory priority, leaves open a multiplicity of opportunities for bureaucratic discretion and corruption. AnnaLee Saxenian's article 'Government and Guanxi: the Chinese software industry in transition' vividly highlights this point although it bears the risk of exaggeration and not taking into consideration the change in China's business culture. As noted by one executive from a famous Chinese home appliance firm, Haier, '...The old concept of sales as managing the distributor relationship through "wine and dine" is not applicable in the current market. Retailers are no longer focused on how much you can drink together, but on how much money you can make for them.'[10]

In contrast with the rapid economic growth has been the slow pace of social programs, such as building the social security net. According to an IBM research report, China's economic growth in the past 25 years has not resulted in better health and healthcare in China. Healthcare has been largely neglected, as the responsibility for providing comprehensive healthcare shifted away from state-owned enterprises (SOEs) and successful rural programs (for example, the 'barefoot doctors') were dismantled without establishing an alternate system. The development of the healthcare sector is now far behind economic development in China. A review of China's key health indicators makes clear the case for change. Life expectancy and infant mortality trends, for example, illustrate that although China's healthcare system has made progress over the last ten years, improvements have slowed recently. Similarly, indicators such as the reported incidence and mortality rates from infectious diseases have increased in recent years. Healthcare expenditures as a percentage of GDP have been increasing in China, but remain low when compared to developed countries and even some other developing countries. For example, China spent 5.8 per cent of its GDP on healthcare in 2002, as compared to 8 per cent by the eight countries of the Organisation for Economic Cooperation and Development (OECD) and 5 per cent or more by other developing countries, such as South Africa (8.7 per cent), Brazil (7.9 per cent) and India (6.1 per cent).[11]

Another problem after 25 years of economic reform has been the ever-increasing inequality of income distribution, which has been hotly debated by China's academics (at the time of writing, the Gini coefficient has now reached 0.4). The success in solving this problem by the government will be critical to social stability and further success of economic and political reform.

In the five decades since the founding of the People's Republic of China in 1949, China has built a sound higher education and vocational training system. In 1981, China roadmapped a higher education system composed of Bachelors, Masters and Doctoral degrees. Starting from the late 1990s, the number of enrolments to universities and colleges has been increasing at a double-digit speed. The number of universities also increased sharply. By the end of 2003, there were 1,552 regular higher education institutions (HEI), an increase of 156, with an enrolment of 11.09 million, 2.05 million more than that in 2002. The HEI entrance rate of 2003 was 17 per cent. This number will continue climbing in the coming decade. Besides higher education, vocational and technical education is also hot in the Chinese market. In 2003, there were 147,000 vocational schools with an enrolment of 5.16 million.

China's technology development environment

Saxenian[12] summarises the evolution of China's science and technology system into three stages: (1) science and technology in the planned economy (1949–1977), (2) abandoning central planning (1978–1992), and (3) market reforms to accelerate science and technology development (after 1992).

In the era of planned economy, China's technological development was under the direct guidance of the government. On the national level, the Ministry of State Planning Commission and the State Science and Technology commission were the major institutions responsible for the control and coordination of all research, development and engineering activities. Research and development was conducted by the state-owned research institutes and hundreds of industrial and local institutes that conducted more applied research and development. The most significant technological achievements of this period were in high priority strategic weapons such as guided missiles and artificial satellites. In this period, China's universities were organised to both create and disseminate basic scientific and technological knowledge, but their focus was primarily on teaching rather than research.

Concurrent with the path of China's economic reform and opening up to the outside world, the second and third stage witnessed more and more market forces in China's science and technology development. In the 1980s and 1990s, the Chinese government initiated several high-profile initiatives and projects in order to enhance the country's innovation capability in science and technology. The most famous '863' plan (named for its approval date of March 1986) allocated approximately 5 billion RMB between 1986 and 2000 to projects designed to monitor Chinese capabilities in the world's high-technology fields such as biotechnology, information technology, energy, robotics, new materials, space, and lasers. In the early 1990s the government invested heavily in accelerating the adoption of IT in key sectors such as the Golden Project (adoption of IT in banking), Golden Bridge (the construction of a national telecommunications backbone and other networks), and Golden Custom (computer networking for foreign trade and other related issues). Another significant project that has fostered the high-technology industrial development zones was the 'Torch Plan' that was proposed by the State Council in the 1980s, with the aim of creating a supportive environment for development of new technology enterprises. The famous high-tech centre Zhongguancun in Beijing, which is sometimes referred to as China's Silicon Valley, showcases the achievement.

China's superior infrastructure is a plus for its software industry development. After more than two decades of rapid economic development, there have been impressive levels of achievement in building the national telecommunications infrastructure and information technology adoption, such as wireless phones and Internet penetration. With the software development delivery model increasingly moving towards outsourcing and offshore services, a robust and reliable telecoms infrastructure has become a priority. Issues such as teledensity are important for enhancing Internet penetration in a country, which in turn will spur the growth of the domestic software and services market as well as other industry segments such as e-commerce. Both China and India have advanced rapidly in their telecommunications industry, but China has a significant advantage. For example, in 2004, China's fixed lines and mobile telephones were at a level of 499 per 1,000 people, almost five times that of India (Table 2.4). Internet penetration and power consumption per capita shows similar differences (Table 2.5 and 2.6).

China's environmental issues

One of the serious negative consequences of China's rapid industrial development has been increased pollution and degradation of natural resources. A World Health Organisation (WHO) report on air quality in 272 cities worldwide concluded that seven of the world's 10 most polluted cities were in China. According to China's own evaluation, two-thirds of the 338 cities for which air-quality data are available are considered polluted – and two-thirds of that figure are moderately or severely so. Respiratory and heart diseases related to air pollution are the leading cause of death in China. Almost all of the nation's rivers are considered polluted to some degree and half of the population lacks access to clean water. By some estimates, every day approximately 300 million residents drink contaminated water. Ninety per cent of urban

Table 2.4 **Fixed lines and mobile telephones (per 1,000 people)**

	2000	2001	2002	2003	2004
China	182	256	328	413	499
India	35	44	52	64	85

Source: World Development Indicators database (*http://devdata.worldbank.org/data-query*).

Table 2.5 **Internet penetration rates (per 1,000 people)**

	2000	2001	2002	2003	2004
China	18	26	46	62	73
India	5	7	16	17	32

Source: World Development Indicators database (*http://devdata.worldbank.org/data-query.*)

Table 2.6 **Electric power consumption (KWH per capita)**

	2000	2001	2002	2003
China	993	1,069	1,184	1,379
India	400	403	417	435

Source: World Development Indicators database (*http://devdata.worldbank.org/data-query.*)

water bodies are severely polluted. Water scarcity also is an issue: for example, severe water scarcity in Northern China is a serious threat to sustained economic growth and the government has begun working on a project for a large-scale diversion of water from the Yangtze River to northern cities, including Beijing and Tianjin. Acid rain falls on 30 per cent of the country. Various studies estimate pollution costs the Chinese economy 7–10 per cent of GDP each year.

China's leaders are increasingly paying attention to the country's severe environmental problems. In 1998, the State Environmental Protection Administration (SEPA) was officially upgraded to a ministry-level agency, reflecting the growing importance the Chinese government places on environmental protection. In recent years, China has strengthened its environmental legislation and made some progress in stemming environmental deterioration. In 2005, China joined the Asia Pacific Partnership on Clean Development, which brings industries and governments together to implement strategies that reduce pollution and address climate change. During the 10th Five-Year Plan, China plans to reduce total emissions by 10 per cent. Beijing in particular is investing heavily in pollution control as part of its campaign to host a successful Olympiad in 2008. Some cities have seen an improvement in air quality in recent years.

China is an active participant in climate change talks and other multilateral environmental negotiations, taking environmental challenges seriously, but pushing for the developed world to help developing countries to a greater extent.

China's legal systems

The government's efforts to promote rule of law are significant and ongoing. After the Cultural Revolution, China's leaders aimed to develop a legal system to restrain abuses of official authority and revolutionary excesses. In 1982, the National People's Congress adopted a new state constitution that emphasised the rule of law under which even party leaders are theoretically held accountable.

Since 1979, when the drive to establish a functioning legal system began, more than 300 laws and regulations, most of them in the economic area, have been promulgated. The use of mediation committees – informed groups of citizens who resolve approximately 90 per cent of China's civil disputes and some minor criminal cases at no cost to the parties – is one innovative device. There are more than 800,000 such committees in both rural and urban areas.

Legal reform became a government priority in the 1990s. Legislation designed to modernise and professionalise the nation's lawyers, judges, and prisons was enacted. The 1994 Administrative Procedure Law allows citizens to sue officials for abuse of authority or malfeasance. In addition, the criminal law and the criminal procedures laws were amended to introduce significant reforms.

One weakness of China's legal systems is its lack of transparency and independency. Although the Chinese constitution states that judicial proceedings are to be free of interference from other government and political identities, judges, courts, and other judicial organs remain under their supervision and dependent on them for funding. The legal obligations of other government entities to enforce or obey court decisions are not adequately established, and court decisions are often ignored as a result.[13]

A western lawyer warns of the apparent schizophrenia in the evolution of law and practice in the Chinese technology sector over the past few years '...The impression of schizophrenia derives, in part, from the lack of transparency in regulation and policymaking: state agencies and actors can (and do) change the rules of the game with little warning: state agencies and actors of different agencies and different levels of government in China are often contradictory. The government is organised around a complicated inner network of personal relationships that do not correspond to a standard organisational chart or Western bureaucracy. In theory the Communist Party controls the government, yet no individual or committee rules in predictable top-down fashion. Decisions are the product of continuous and complex two-way negotiations between individuals in different ministries (horizontally) and levels (vertically) of government. These internal debates remain inaccessible to all but select insiders.'[14]

In recent years, under domestic and international pressure, the government has tightened its enforcement of IPR protection. By no means coincidental with Chinese President Hu Jintao's visit to Microsoft's headquarters in Seattle in 2006, China's top computer manufacturers pledged to install legitimate copies of operating systems. This act has been lauded by Microsoft as a turning point for the company's 14 years of history in the Chinese market.

It can be expected that the Chinese authorities' commitment under their WTO agreements will help improve judicial enforcement of contracts and other business codes, including those governing intellectual property and counterfeiting.

The impact of WTO accession on China's IT industry

One milestone in China's economic and social development was its accession to the WTO in late 2001. After years of negotiation, an agreement was reached that required China to adhere more closely to international economic norms. China made concessions that would further open and liberalise its policies to 'better integrate in the world economy and offer a more predictable environment for trade and foreign investment in accordance with WTO rules.' Among the changes, China agreed to reduce tariffs to lower levels, eliminate remaining dual-pricing practices, repeal price controls used to protect domestic industries, do away with export subsidies on agricultural products, and afford equal trade rights to all WTO members. China retained exclusive state trading rights for key products such as cereals, tobacco, fuels, and minerals. It also maintained certain restrictions affecting transportation and distribution of goods within the country. Otherwise, the government agreed to phase out (or minimise), between 2001 and 2010, many of the regulatory barriers previously faced by foreign companies in China. By 2004 (just two years after joining the WTO), tariffs had been reduced on 5300 commodities, with the average tariff falling from 15.3 per cent to 11 per cent. Some 2,300 trade-related laws and regulations were also amended, and another 830 had been abolished.[15]

Through its accession to the WTO, China has committed to wide-ranging reforms affecting trade in IT and telecommunications equipment that should result in better access for foreign suppliers to the Chinese market. These reforms include agreeing to sign the Information Technology Agreement (ITA), thereby eliminating tariffs on all products covered by it; to allow imports and distribution of most products, particularly those covered by the ITA, into any part of China; and to remove quotas and local content, technology transfer, and export performance requirements. China also agreed to allow an increased level of foreign investment and/or open a larger geographic area to foreign participation through a staged implementation plan for its IT, Internet, and telecommunications services markets. For example, in the telecommunications services area, it will allow 50 per cent foreign participation in value-added services two years after accession, 49 per cent in mobile voice and data services five years after accession, and 49 per cent in domestic basic services six years after accession. The Chinese government has further committed to undertake the pro-competitive obligations contained in the Reference Paper of the WTO

Agreement on Basic Telecommunications Services, such as establishing an independent regulator, defining interconnection rights, and prohibiting anti-competitive practices. China's accession to the WTO should stimulate greater foreign competition and investment in China's e-commerce market as well, that will spur the development and introduction of more efficient mechanisms for online payment, delivery, and security.

The accession of China to the WTO marks an important milestone along the reform path China has been following for more than twenty years, rather than a new direction. China has been liberalising its international trade and investment policies since the mid-1980s and is now as open as some present WTO members. Although China stands to gain significantly from the opening of its export markets under the terms of its accession, the depth and breadth of its commitment to liberalise access to its domestic economy are acknowledged to be more extensive than those agreed to by previous adherents to the WTO. This willingness reflects the fact that opening to international markets promotes market discipline, access to technology, and other qualities that have been important goals of domestic economic reforms. In this respect, WTO entry is a complementary aspect of the next phase of China's reforms.

Conclusions

After several decades of economic reform and opening to the outside world, China is on its way toward a modern society based on rule of law. The 11–5 economic development plan has set a new agenda on the creation of a harmonious society, which will have some further important implications for China's economic development and social transformation. The PESTEL analysis indicates that the Chinese software industry exists in an unprecedented environment of stimulation and support.

Notes

1. 'What's to stop India and China', *Economist*, October 27, 2005.
2. 'Democracy's drawbacks', *Economist*, October 27, 2005.
3. 'The competitive advantage of China', the Stanford Graduate School of Business, case # IB-57, 2004, p. 6.
4. Saxenian, A.L. (2003) 'Government and Guanxi: the Chinese software industry in transition', CNEM working paper: 1.

5. OECD (2002) 'China in the world economy: the domestic policy challenges', *OECD Synthesis report*, 5–6.
6. Saxenian, op. cit.: 13.
7. If not noted otherwise, the information in this section is mainly based on the US Department of State background report note at *http://www.infoplease.com/country/profiles/china.html*
8. This section is mainly based on the information in 'The competitive advantage of China', op. cit.
9. Lee, K.-F. *Making IT in China*. Available at *http://www.guanxithebook.com/how_to_make_it_in_china.html*
10. 'Haier: taking a Chinese company global', HBS case # 9-706-401, Boston, MA: Harvard Business School Publishing; p. 6.
11. IBM (2006) 'Healthcare in China: towards greater access, efficiency and quality', IBM Institute for Business Value.
12. Saxenian, op. cit.
13. OECD, op. cit.
14. Saxenian, op. cit.: 2.
15. 'The competitive advantage of China', op. cit., pp. 5–6.

3

India: a PESTEL analysis

Introduction

In the last three decades India has gained a prominent position on the world business map due to its emergence as a leading 'software nation'. In fact, so phenomenal has the rise of the Indian software industry been that it is often considered as a notable economic development of the last century. What began with the supply of skilled software professionals to the United States in the 1970s came to be the world's fastest growing software industry over the next three decades, known globally for its superior software capability and leading to a new identity for India. After a brief overview, this chapter presents a PESTEL analysis of the Indian software industry.[1]

Overview of India's software industry

India, with its 29 states and seven union territories, is the world's largest democracy, and has a population in excess of one billion growing at the rate of 1.5 per cent every year. With a GDP of approximately US $754.8 billion,[2] India achieved a GDP growth of 8.4 per cent year-on-year in 2005–2006, making it one of the fastest growing economies in the world. In the World Economic Forum's Global Competitiveness Survey 2005, India achieved a rank of 50 as measured by growth competitiveness index, and ranked 31st in terms of the business competitiveness index.[3]

Ever since its beginnings, the Indian software industry has grown at a spectacular rate. It has achieved an average growth rate of more than 40 per cent over the past few years despite an economic slowdown that affected worldwide markets. In the financial year ending March 2006, the Indian software industry recorded aggregate revenue of US $29.6 billion, of which US $23.6 billion came from software exports.

Table 3.1 presents the composition and growth of India's software industry over the last three financial years, whereas Table 3.2 shows the employment opportunities the industry has generated during the period.[4]

As can be seen from Table 3.1, the Indian software industry is largely an export-driven industry, providing customised software and IT services to other countries. Several factors have contributed to the unprecedented growth of the Indian software industry, key among them are a vast, English-speaking high-quality technical talent pool, attractive cost structures, favourable government policies, a world-class educational system, process excellence, social networks and, of course, fortuitous circumstances that offered growing global market opportunities. As the industry gained deeper market penetration, it successfully leveraged its capabilities and experiential knowledge and strengthened its comparative advantage in the global software industry through its offshore outsourcing business model.

Table 3.1   **Composition and growth of India's software industry**

In billion US $	FY 2004	FY 2005	FY 2006
Software and IT services[1]	**10.4**	**13.5**	**17.7**
Exports	7.3	10	13.3
Domestic	3.1	3.5	4.4
Research and development (R&D) and Engineering services (including Outsourced Product Development)	**2.9**	**3.7**	**4.7**
Exports	2.5	3.1	4.0
Domestic	0.4	0.6	0.7
IT enabled and BPO services	**3.4**	**5.2**	**7.2**
Exports	3.1	4.6	6.3
Domestic	0.3	0.6	0.9
Total software and services revenues	**16.7**	**22.6**	**29.6**
Total Exports Revenue	**12.9**	**17.7**	**23.6**
Total Domestic Revenue[2]	**3.8**	**4.9**	**6.0**

Source: NASSCOM.

[1] Software and IT Services includes (a) project oriented services such as IT consulting, systems integrations, custom software development and maintenance, independent verification and validation services, and network consulting and services (b) IT outsourcing, application outsourcing, and infrastructure management (c) training and support.

[2] An accurate assessment of India's domestic software and IT services market is difficult because the published figures for the domestic market include software products and package revenues as well.

| Table 3.2 | | Employment growth in India's software industry | |

Table 3.2   Employment growth in India's software industry

Employment segment	FY 2004	FY 2005	FY 2006
Software and IT services	614,000	741,000	878,000
ITES – BPO	253,000	316,000	415,000
Total	867,000	5,107,000	1,293,000

Source: NASSCOM.

Currently, the Indian software and IT services industry has an estimated 6,000 companies in India, of which approximately 60 per cent are domestic and nearly 40 per cent are MNCs.[5] The Indian software industry comprises three types of companies: Indian software and IT service companies, captive software and IT service centres of multinational companies, and entrepreneurial software start-ups. Table 3.3 captures a sample of leading Indian and multi-national companies that constitute the Indian software and IT service industry. Besides these, companies such as General Electric, Honeywell, Yahoo!, Robert Bosch, DaimlerChrysler and so on have major research and development presences in India. Many leading financial institutions also have their equity/financial research centres in India. Most of the software companies are located in geographical clusters across India – Delhi and neighbouring NOIDA and Gurgaon in the north; Bangalore, Chennai and Hyderabad in the south; Mumbai and Pune in the west; and Kolkata in the east.

Interestingly, data from NASSCOM[6] as well as *Dataquest* Magazine[7], which creates an annual ranking for firms in the Indian IT industry,

Table 3.3   Sample list of companies in India's software industries

Company	Country of origin	Nature of work
Accenture	USA	Consulting, software and IT services, BPO
Adobe Systems	USA	Software product development, software product sales
Cap Gemini	France	Software and IT services
Cisco systems	USA	Networking product software
Cognizant Technologies Solutions	USA	Software solutions and services, IT services

Table 3.3	Sample list of companies in India's software industries (*Cont'd*)

Company	Country of origin	Nature of work
Google	USA	Software R&D
HCL Technologies	India	Software and IT services, R&D services BPO
Hewlett Packard	USA	Software development, BPO
Huawei Technologies	China	Telecoms product software development
IBM	USA	Consulting, software and IT services, software product development, research, hardware and software sales
Infosys Technologies Ltd	India	Consulting, software and IT services, R&D services, BPO
Intel	USA	Chip design
Lucent Technologies	USA	Telecoms product software development
Microsoft	USA	Software product sales, software product development, research
Motorola	USA	Telecoms software development
Oracle	USA	Software product development, software product sales
Patni Computer Systems	India	Software and IT services, BPO
Samsung	Korea	Telecoms and consumer electronics software development
SAP	Germany	Software product development, software product sales
Satyam Computer Services	India	Consulting, software and IT services, R&D services, BPO
Siemens	Germany	Telecoms, medical, transportation, and consumer electronics software development
Symantec	USA	Software product development, software product sales
Tata Consultancy Services	India	Consulting, software and IT services, R&D services, BPO
Texas Instruments	USA	Chip design, DSP software
Wipro Technologies Ltd	India	Consulting, software and IT services, R&D services, BPO

Sources: STPI, NASSCOM and *Dataquest* Magazine.

indicates that nearly 45 per cent of the industry's revenue is generated by the top 20 firms.[8] Also, it is important to recognise that the Indian software industry is comprised of both Indian firms as well as subsidiaries of foreign-based firms.

The software industry has had a significant impact on India's economy, contributing an estimated 4.8 per cent to its GDP in 2005–2006. Today, India is a leading destination for offshore software development and IT services, accounting for nearly 60 per cent of the global offshore software and IT services market as well as approximately 50 per cent of the global BPO (business process outsourcing) industry. An estimated 878,000 professionals are employed by the software industry in India. However, currently India accounts for less than 3 per cent market share in the global software industry, which suggests a huge growth opportunity for the Indian software industry.

The genesis of the Indian software industry can be traced to the early 1970s, when a few companies started providing skilled software professionals to companies overseas – often referred to as 'onsite services'. The success of this early business model of staff augmentation and the attractive proposition it offered has been a key driver for the evolution and growth of the software services. Later, encouraged by government policies and the business need to be profitable and offer better cost–value propositions to clients, the industry transitioned to primarily an offshore based service delivery model. This transition was enabled by the industry's ability to instil confidence among its client base through proven technical capability, quality process certifications, and effective management practices for handling remote work alongside an improved networking and communication infrastructure for cross-border work. The dot-com boom and the Y2K problem were also instrumental in speeding up the transition as they resulted in valuable relationship capital for the Indian firms in addition to the demonstration of their ability to offer scale advantage. The economic downturn of 1999–2000, which made corporations highly cost conscious, further accelerated the transition to the offshore outsourcing model.

India's software industry is primarily a service-intensive industry with a strong focus on exports. There are several reasons for the industry's chosen focus on services (as opposed to products and packages). First of all, a software products business requires large up-front investment and could also be risky, whereas a service business requires less up-front capital and ensures a steady revenue stream. There were also such factors as lack of opportunities for software products as the IT market was not well developed domestically, and products for global markets could not be developed without proximity to target markets. In addition, the government policy that provided incentives for exports encouraged companies to pursue service businesses. Moreover, in the early days of the software industry there was a lack of IPR awareness, and the threat of software piracy was very high. This meant that piracy could prevent companies from appropriating copyright fees on software product innovations. More recently, some software product businesses have emerged with good potential for expansion into global markets, although software services continue to be an attractive focus area for Indian software companies owing to good demand and less risk.

India's software industry: a PESTEL analysis[9]

India's political environment

India is the world's largest democracy. The term of the Indian parliament is five years. Interestingly, India has had five general elections since 1989, resulting each time in the formation of a fragile coalition government. Since the last general election in May 2005, the Congress party has dominated the United Progressive Alliance coalition, led by the Prime Minister Dr. Manmohan Singh, which has been in power. During the period 1998–2004, the BJP-led National Democratic Alliance was in power. However, irrespective of the number of elections and the various political parties that assumed power, there has been a strong government focus on the software industry. As a result, the software industry has significantly benefited from several policy-induced changes.

The software sector has significantly benefited from the reforms that the Indian government gradually implemented over a span of two decades, particularly from the policy measures pertaining to de-regulation and economic liberalisation. From a policy perspective, India really 'discovered' the huge potential the software industry offered, and gradually evolved its policy to suit the software and IT sector. To that extent, calling India's policy for the software industry evolutionary would not be inappropriate. To start with, the software policy evolved alongside hardware policy, with the government attempting to ensure a tight coupling between them. However, the real impetus for the Indian software industry came when the software policy was decoupled from the hardware policy.

During the early 1970s and early 1980s, government policies were protectionist in nature and stemmed from an interest in achieving indigenous hardware capability. Hardware imports were allowed only on the condition that the price of the hardware would be recovered within five years through foreign exchange earnings. The foreign exchange rules were quite limiting and cumbersome, and the customs procedures were quite complicated. In fact, the Foreign Exchange Regulation Act (FERA) of 1973 restricted any foreign firm's interest in doing business in India to only a 40 per cent minority stake. In 1976, the government took initial measures to liberalise the policy for the software sector and provided incentives for software exports by setting up export processing zones (EPZs), and instituting mechanisms for faster clearance of software export applications. Import duties on hardware were also reduced and, while the government allowed imports of hardware for the purposes of software development, by and large its interest in promoting indigenous hardware influenced most of its policy decisions. In 1984, the government instituted a new computer policy under which the import procedures were greatly simplified and access to foreign exchange for software firms was made easier.

The real impetus for the Indian software industry, however, came in 1986 when the government recognised the potential of the software industry and decoupled all policies governing software from the hardware-centred policies by instituting an exclusive software policy. Under this policy, import of hardware for the purposes of software export was exempt from duty, but imported software attracted a duty of 60 per cent of the value. In 1988, the government introduced the most significant policy measure by announcing the establishment of the Software Technology Parks of India (STPI) – an autonomous body under the Department of Electronics meant to encourage and support export-oriented software firms. STPI, in addition to offering a tax-free status for five years within the first eight years of operation, provided office space, computing equipment, and access to high-speed satellite communication links. STPI also served as a 'single window' organisation for import certifications, project approvals, training support, and software valuation.

In 1991, when the full-fledged reform and liberalisation process in India began, the government instituted a New Economic Policy aimed at devaluation and partial convertibility of the Rupee, abolished the tax imposed on foreign exchange for international travel, and reduced telecom charges for satellite links among other benefits such as removal of export obligations for Software Technology Parks. During the period 1993–1999 software exports under the STPI scheme were exempt from income tax and this benefit will continue to be available until the year 2009.

In 1998, the government set up a National Taskforce on IT and Software Development with a view to address the bottlenecks the sector faced, and to give a boost to the industry. In 2000, the government established an IT Act that provided a legal framework for e-commerce, allowed electronic document filing, and recognised digital signatures. In 1999, the Indian government formulated the National Telecom Policy that embedded several steps towards liberalisation of the telecom sector. These reforms included reduction in the licence fee for telecom operators, introduction of more competition, addressing regulatory concerns, reduction in long-distance call tariffs, installation of a unified licensing regime, but more importantly a significantly improved communication infrastructure and low-price, high-quality network bandwidth. In 2005, it further liberalised the telecom sector by allowing an FDI to the extent of 74 per cent, up from its existing 49 per cent limit.

From the history of the growth of the Indian software industry, viewed in the light of the policy reforms, it is evident that the political instability, stemming largely from coalition governments, has not impeded the reforms process in any noticeable way. On the contrary, every political party that has led the government has been receptive to the demands of the software industry lobbies. To that extent, the government played a catalytic role in the shaping up and growth of the Indian software industry. The policy reforms in the telecom sector have also undoubtedly been instrumental in facilitating the growth of the software industry in India.

India's economic development

The Indian software industry has grown at a CAGR of more than 55 per cent during 1993–1999 and more than 30 per cent during 2000–2005, and has shown a remarkable resilience to shocks and economic downturns. The strong export focus continues to expand and the domestic market has also shown a steady growth. With a US $800 billion global software and IT services market, which is estimated to grow at the rate of 7 per cent per annum in the next five years,[10] and with increasing focus on managing costs, streamlining business processes, and achieving faster cycle times, India's exports-dominated software outsourcing industry only stands to gain.

Today, most of the Fortune 500 companies source their software needs from India. Many leading Indian software companies are listed in major foreign stock exchanges, and have significant cash reserves. Currently, the Indian software industry accounts for nearly 60 per cent of the global market share for offshore software and IT services. However, India's share of the global IT industry is less than 3 per cent, which suggests a huge growth potential for the industry. Traditionally the export-oriented Indian software industry has been largely aligned to the US markets, earning as much as 70 per cent of its revenues from the US. However, the Asia-Pacific and European regions offer huge market potential for the Indian software industry, and most firms are now intensely pursuing these markets to secure future growth. Table 3.4 shows the distribution of the revenues of the Indian software industry from various regions during 2005–2006[11].

Besides continued growth in software exports and IT services, the Indian software industry is also witnessing growth in IT spending in the domestic markets in line with the overall economic boom in the country. This means that the domestic market also offers compelling growth opportunities for the Indian software industry. In addition, many Indian software service companies have upgraded themselves to address the more lucrative engineering and R&D services space, deriving further export revenues from the R&D budgets of large technology companies as well as entrepreneurial ventures.

The overall economic situation in India is also quite favourable for the software industry. India has a sound and growing financial and banking sector. Capital markets have been significantly reformed but are highly regulated. The manufacturing sector is also growing in strength, which means that the sector will present handsome opportunities for the software and IT sector. During the financial year April 2005–March 2006, India received an FDI inflow of nearly US $6 billion, of which an estimated US $1.5 billion was related to the software and IT services sector.[12] Currently, India is one of the top three preferred global destinations for foreign direct investment, thanks to the government's liberal policies for attracting FDI.

Table 3.4	Indian software industry's revenue earning per region
Region	**Revenue (%)**
Americas	65
Europe	24
Asia-Pacific and Australia	7 (including 3% from Japan)
Rest of the World	4

Source: NASSCOM.

India offers a huge emerging market and in recognition of this, many Indian companies are focusing on innovation and local market relevance. In fact, the economic opportunities for the software industry in India are so compelling that during 2005–2006 many major global corporations announced significant investments in India. Microsoft, for example, announced an investment of US $1.7 billion, whereas Intel announced an investment decision of US $1.05 billion, IBM US $6 billion, AMD US $3 billion, and Cisco US $1.1 billion among others.[13]

Unlike the early days, and especially since 1999, there has been an easy availability of capital for the software sector. In addition to the funds from financial institutions, availability of venture capital funding significantly promoted entrepreneurial activities in the software sector, diversifying the footprint of the Indian software industry. In the year 2005–2006, there was flow of an estimated US $2 billion in venture capital into India. Many NRIs (non-resident Indians) also extended 'angel funding' to entrepreneurial ventures in the software sector.

While the software sector is quite buoyant, and even though the cumulative impact of the reforms since 1991 has been substantial, the overall economic growth in India is still somewhat constrained by a large trade deficit. Software exports have contributed to addressing the trade deficit, but high oil prices and strong domestic demand have a significant negative impact. In addition, particularly for the software industry, fluctuating exchange rates (US Dollar versus Rupee conversion) is a problem because of its large share of export earnings.

India's society (some socio-cultural factors)

The very nature of the software services business is people intensive, and the Indian software industry has gained considerably from an abundant technical resource pool that exists in the country. The educational system in India produces an estimated 441,000 engineering graduates every year, of which nearly 246,000 graduate with a major in electrical, electronics and computing sciences.[14] Many Indian universities offer master-level degrees in computer science (MSc) or computer applications (MCA).

The government has also responded to the manpower needs of the software industry by increasing the number of its elite Indian Institutes of Technology and setting up six innovative Indian Institutes of Information Technology exclusively focused on providing specialised and advanced IT skills. Many companies have tie-ups with overseas universities for advanced training and education for their employees. In addition, many foreign universities have entered the Indian education sector, offering various certification and degree programs aligned to the needs of the software and IT services industry. Industry bodies such as NASSCOM have entered into a memorandum of understanding with the University Grants Commission in India for faculty development, with a view to address the manpower capacity and quality needs of the software industry. Leading companies such as Infosys Technologies have launched programs to actively work with engineering colleges to improve curriculum relevance for the industry as well as initiate various measures to improve output quality.

In addition, the software industry has witnessed a remarkable public sector–private sector partnership, with the private sector responding very well to the needs of the software industry. For example, companies such as NIIT and Aptech, through their well-designed computer software training programs, have prepared a large pool of professionals for meeting the manpower needs of the software industry.

English is widely spoken in India, and most of the science and technology education in universities is imparted in the English language. English language proficiency has been remarkably helpful for the Indian software industry, especially as the service-intensive industry needed to work with multinational teams. Currently, the Indian software industry employs an estimated 878,000 professionals and provides indirect employment to nearly 2.5 million people. Nearly 70 per cent of the professionals employed are men, whereas 30 per cent are women. The median age of software professionals is 28 years.[15]

The job-seeking talent pool has very favourably considered career opportunities in the software industry because of the intellectually stimulating nature of software jobs, relatively higher income levels, career growth opportunities due to a burgeoning industry, opportunities for international exposure, and also because of its environmental friendliness. In addition, the wealth creation opportunities offered by software companies through employee stock options are also a matter of major appeal to the prospective employee pool.

Today, software jobs are considered to be dream jobs in the Indian job market, and there is very stiff competition among companies to attract people. Indian software companies such as Infosys Technologies, Tata Consultancy Services and Wipro Technologies represent the face of the new India. Many of the Indian software companies have also connected with the larger society through their corporate social outreach programmes, thus improving their brand recall in society at large.

Media reports are abuzz about the glorious performance of the software sector. As a result of all these factors, software jobs are considered very prestigious as well as lucrative in Indian society, leading to greater numbers of people seeking jobs in the software industry.

The Indian software industry has also benefited from the Indian Diaspora. Many Indians engaged in entrepreneurial activities in the West, especially in the USA's Silicon Valley, either returned home to continue their entrepreneurial pursuits or expanded the footprint of their entrepreneurial ventures to India to leverage its software talent. In addition, the social networks that were established as a result of the Indian Diaspora also catalysed software business growth. Organisations such as The Indus Entrepreneurs (TiE) provided platforms for formation of social networks, and also catalysed the growth of entrepreneurial activities in the Indian software sector.

Finally, the Indian software industry has also benefited from a unique dimension of its social and cultural fabric – flexibility. Leveraging its ability to deal with diversity and flexibility, which is a typical characteristic of the Indian culture, the Indian software professionals not only adapted themselves to the demand of global work that the export-oriented software services required, but also quickly mastered fast-changing and emerging technologies. This combination of effectively handling diversity and demonstrating flexibility has been a significant, but often unnoticed, factor responsible for the growth of the Indian software industry.

India's technology development environment

Given the predominant export focus of the Indian software industry, traditionally, technology came from outside – from the clients the companies served. By and large, R&D has been non-existent in the Indian software industry until late 1990s. For executing software services contracts, all that the industry needed was a range of technical skills and a superior software delivery capability. This is where the Indian software industry has shown remarkable performance. The industry as a whole has consistently demonstrated its ability to quickly migrate to new platforms and adapt to new technologies, aligning its growth with technology waves. Towards this end, the industry has invested considerably in education and training, as well as in certifying its professionals in key technology platforms such as .NET and J2EE, and technology areas such as data warehousing, networking, and security. In addition, the industry has also invested heavily in quality and project management certifications such as CQA, CSQE, PMI and the like.

From mainframe systems to client server technology; from Unix to Windows and Linux platforms; from closed systems to open systems, e-commerce and Internet-based systems, the Indian software industry has been quick in ramping up technical skills and building a large pool of technically-proficient staff. In addition, the Indian software industry has also been quick in assimilating emerging technologies such as mobility, web services and service-oriented architecture, and in using new software development environments and productivity tools. The English language proficiency has helped to keep it up to date with constantly changing software technologies.

In order to address the need for productivity and delivery efficiency, companies in the Indian software industry made significant investments in process excellence and acquired strong project management skills. Most leading companies have developed sophisticated project management, process automation, and knowledge management tools that give them an edge over their competitors. Almost all software services companies hold quality certifications such as ISO 9000 and Software CMM. In fact, India has the world's largest number of Software CMM Level 4 and 5 companies. As a result, Indian software industry players have acquired an ability to manage large, complex software projects in a predictable manner. With years of working with clients in various verticals, the companies also have developed substantial and highly valuable domain skills.

The linkage between the industry and academia by and large has been rather poor though, and it is not clear if the universities have had any impact on technological upgrading in the Indian software industry except in providing a well-trained talent pool. Most of the technological upgrading has happened through closer interactions with clients, through the technology alliances the Indian companies have set up with leading technology vendors, and through a growing MNC R&D base in India. In fact, the role of MNCs in the technological upgrading of the Indian software industry has been significant. MNCs not only contributed to technological knowledge accumulation within the industry, often as a result of the local ecosystem and labour movements, but also catalysed entrepreneurial ventures in the software sector.

As mentioned above, the R&D intensity has been rather low in the predominantly service-oriented software industry. However, with increasing global competition and a quest for value migration, and the innovation opportunities offered by an emerging market such as India, all leading Indian software companies have invested in developing in-house R&D capabilities, while simultaneously leveraging their alliances for access to technological know-how. This trend is complemented by a growing MNC R&D base in India. Even though currently, the cumulative R&D spend of the Indian software industry is less than 1 per cent of the revenues, the overall R&D base is expanding.

Many Indian firms have focused on niche areas such as animation and games software, which requires highly specialised technical and creative skills. Yet many others, such as Bangalore-based Wipro Technologies, capitalising on their investments in building domain knowledge, have strategically focused on providing high-value R&D services in areas such as telecoms and chip design, operating 'labs-for-hire' for their clients. In addition, a new breed of companies such as Ittiam Systems, ImpulseSoft, and Sasken, that are in the business of licensing advanced technologies in specific technology domains, have emerged onto the scene.

The government for its part has also installed programmes to facilitate technology development and setting up of a national innovation ecosystem, emphasising indigenous technology development. Towards this end, the government provides full tax relief on in-house R&D expenditure and also gives full tax exemption on royalties earned through exports of indigenously-developed technologies. The department of scientific and industrial research runs a programme for technological self-reliance and supports R&D projects in the industry. The government also established the National Research Development Corporation (NRDC), with a view to transfer technology from R&D labs to the industry. However, the impact of such government initiatives on the software industry is unclear.

India's environmental issues

The environmental factors have been largely in favour of the Indian software industry. There has been a growing demand for global offshore outsourcing backed by constant governmental, educational and societal support. And even though in recent times there has been an increasing political backlash against offshoring, looking at the growth trends it is safe to conclude that the Indian software industry has not really been affected. On the contrary, the backlash has only heightened the visibility of the Indian software industry globally.

The Indian software industry is facing growing competition from other countries, and the rising wages are gradually eroding the cost advantage that Indian companies have hitherto leveraged. Therefore, there is a clear imperative for Indian software companies to innovate and demonstrate continued value. Indian firms have responded by increasing their R&D

focus, migrating to higher-value services such as consulting, package implementation, and offering technology-based business solutions.

Interestingly, many Indian companies have embarked on globalising into other low-cost nations, particularly China, to expand their capacity and tap into local markets. Indian companies have also been acquiring companies overseas to obtain technology and domain know-how as well as to secure customer and employee bases. Encouraged by the government's favourable policies and a potentially large market, many MNCs have been expanding their presence in India and growing their R&D base. Their presence has catalysed the capability build-up in the Indian software industry but fuelled the war for talent.

A striking feature of the Indian software industry is the fact that it has been free of any union troubles. Most software firms are professionally managed with transparent business and human resource management practices. Many leading Indian companies such as Infosys Technologies have set global benchmarks in corporate governance. Even the Indian Ministry of Company Affairs has established focus on corporate governance along with many industry bodies such as the Confederation of Indian Industries, the Institute of Chartered Accountants of India and the Institute of Company Secretaries of India.

Although there have been frequent mentions of risks such as terrorism and border security tensions, in reality these have not had any impact on the Indian software industry. In fact, most cities that have a concentration of software companies are far from India's geo-political borders and hence they are quite insulated from any security tensions that may arise because of India's relationships with its neighbours.

However, one factor that could potentially hinder India's sustained growth in the software industry is the buckling urban infrastructure that is indeed becoming a bottleneck. Further, even though there are many big cities in India with a high concentration of activities related to international trade, India does not yet have even a single international-class airport! Additionally, fluctuation in valuation of the Rupee and an employee turnover of 10–35 per cent are some of the main causes for concern. The Indian legal system, which often takes long periods for resolution of disputes, is a bottleneck, too, especially in the wake of a growing importance for IPR protection.

India's legal systems

From a legal angle, there are two key areas that warrant consideration in the Indian software industry: protection of intellectual property rights and data security and privacy. Countering software piracy has been an important thrust area in the Indian software industry, whereas with the growth of offshore outsourcing, ensuring security and privacy of data has emerged as an important business necessity. The overall IP orientation in the industry has developed only recently, and many leading companies have intensified their efforts to protect their intellectual assets through patents and copyright registrations.

India does not recognise software patents,[16] and so intellectual property rights related to software are covered by the Indian Copyright Act 1957, which is perhaps one of the most stringent copyright laws in the world. The act was revised in 1994 to incorporate some major changes, which were brought into effect in 1995. In 1999 the Copyright Act was further amended to make it TRIPS compliant.[17] India, however, is not a signatory to the WIPO copyright treaty of 2002. The Indian Copyright Act also includes issuance of the International Copyright Order, which extends provisions of the copyright act to the nationals of all WTO member countries.

Under the Indian Copyright Act, making or distributing copies of copyrighted software without proper or specific authorisation, except for temporary back-up, is considered illegal. An infringer can be tried in both the civil and criminal courts, and is liable to face a jail term of up to three years in addition to punitive cash penalties. However, the Indian Copyright Act does not provide any protection against reverse engineering.

Even though India has had very tough copyright laws, software piracy has been a major problem, which means that enforcement of the laws has been weak. The revenue loss due to piracy in the software products business during 2005–2006 is estimated to be in the range of US $600 million to US $1 billion.[18] Often, India's shying away from the software product and package business is attributed to the weak enforcement of intellectual property rights, which only meant revenue erosion for companies pursuing product-based business strategy. By contrast, and quite interestingly, there is a belief that availability of pirated or illegal software has actually given rise to an increased penetration of computers.

Irrespective of the view one takes, software piracy has been a problem that both the industry and the government recognised as a major hindrance to the growth of the software industry. This recognition culminated in a substantial commitment by the government and the industry bodies to counter piracy. For example, the apex software industry body, NASSCOM, along with the Business Software Alliance, launched a major campaign to eliminate piracy and also conducted anti-piracy raids. Additionally, in order to curb piracy, the government removed import duty on software. There is evidence that these efforts have paid off and that the extent of piracy has decreased.

In order to address the concerns related to data security and privacy, the government of India instituted the IT Act of 2000. This Act, however, does not have any direct provisions to deal with data security and privacy, but has several proxy laws and policies covering download, access, misuse, and extraction of data, including hacking and wrongful damage to data. Many Indian software companies have also responded by complying with major information security standards, and obtained certifications such as BS 7799. The government of India has also established an Information Security Technology Development Council (ISTDC) to augment industry's efforts to address data security and privacy related requirements.

Interest in patents has hitherto been low in the Indian software industry. Traditionally, Indian software companies have not been active in filing patents and seeking IP protection. This is primarily because most Indian software companies focused on providing software services, which largely consisted of custom software design and implementation for clients. Moreover, by filing for patents and seeking IP protection, the Indian software companies did not want to instil a sense of competition among their clients. This meant that by design their work did not cause any conflict with their clients' intellectual property interests. Other factors such as the high cost of filing and defending patents and inability to commercially exploit intellectual property have also contributed to a shying away from patenting.

However, with the intensification of competition and emergence of India as a major market, there is a growing patent culture as well as a strongly-evolving patent regime. In their quest for global competitiveness, the Indian companies are striving to move up the value chain and are increasingly approaching their competitive positioning with intellectual-property-based differentiation. This has given rise to a keen interest in patenting activity. Also, a growing MNC presence has given a substantial impetus to the patent culture. Even though the number of patents filed by Indian companies is still small when compared to the MNC software subsidiaries in India, evidence indicates that patenting will become a key element of Indian software companies' innovation and competitive strategy. Table 3.5 provides information on patents filed by the MNC subsidiaries and Indian companies during 2004–2005 and 2005–2006.[19]

Table 3.5	Patent filing by firms in the Indian software industry					
Patents filed by MNC subsidiaries in India			Patents filed by Indian software firms			
Company	2004–05	2005–06	Company	2004–05	2005–06	
Microsoft	40	70	Infosys Technologies	0	20	
Symantec	47	57	Ramco	16	16	
ST Microelectronics	62	37	Tata Consultancy Services	16	13	
Freescale	710	16	Sasken Communications	5	5	
Flextronics	2	4	MindTree Technologies	1	2	
Cadence	1	0	Subex Systems	0	2	
Texas Instruments	35	0	i-flex	1	1	

Source: *Dataquest* Magazine, 15 July 2006

As things stand today, most software companies from India seek US or PCT patents, a choice that is perhaps based on the territory of their competition. Specialised software service companies such as Sasken Communications derive nearly 15 per cent of their revenues through licensing of their intellectual property. Companies with business models based exclusively on IP licensing have also arrived on the Indian software industry scene. A case in point is Ittiam Systems, a Bangalore-based company that develops and licences DSP software IP blocks to technology companies globally.

Conclusions

Since its beginning in the late seventies, the Indian software industry has grown by leaps and bounds as testified by standard economic indicators such as growth in sales, employment, and export volumes. While the genesis of the Indian software industry can be traced to fortuitous circumstances and an evolutionary approach characterised by experimentation, its growth is certainly attributable to a deliberate strategy supported by a host of hard and soft factors. Among the hard factors, India's education system, vast science and engineering talent pool, economic reforms and government's facilitative policies, and opportunities in the global IT marketplace have been the key. Whereas, the ability to adapt to changing technologies and effectively handle a variety of customer idiosyncrasies, the Indian Diaspora and the associated social networks, customer relationship capital, and the cultural flexibility have been the key among the soft factors.

Notes

1. This chapter relies on secondary sources of information as well as the author's own research.
2. Source: The Economist Intelligence Unit.
3. World Economic Forum (*http://www.weforum.org*): Global Competitiveness Survey 2005.
4. Source: National Association of Software and Services Companies in India (NASSCOM); see *http://www.nasscom.in*. Unless otherwise mentioned, most of the data is based on NASSCOM reports and publications.
5. Sources: STPI, NASSCOM and *Dataquest*.
6. NASSCOM is the apex software industry body in India. Useful information on the Indian software industry as well as on doing business in India is available at its web site, *http://www.nasscom.in*
7. *Dataquest* magazine (*http://www.dqindia.com*), a fortnightly publication, is a useful source of information on the Indian software industry. Every year, it publishes a comprehensive account on the various sectors of the Indian IT industry under a series of 'DQ Top 20' special issues, which also includes details on companies.
8. For *Dataquest's* annual ranking of the firms in the Indian software industry, see *http://www.dqindia.com*
9. Most scholarly work on the Indian software industry has been undertaken with an economic and policy analysis perspective. There is no significant work that is available that provides a coverage on the Indian software industry from a managerial perspective. Major works from an economics and policy analysis perspective include: Heeks, R. (1996) *India's Software Industry*. New Delhi: Sage Publications; Arora, A., Arunachalam, V.S., Asundi, J. and Fernandes, R. (1999) 'The Indian software industry', report to the Alfred Sloan Foundation, Carnegie Mellon University; available at *http://www.heinz.cmu.edu/project/india*. Athreye, S. (2005) 'The Indian software industry and its evolving service capability', *Industrial and Corporate Change*, 14(3): 393–418 provides an economic and policy analysis view on India's software services industry integrated with a dynamic capabilities perspective. The only notable exception is Banerjee, P. (2004) *The Indian Software Industry: Business Strategy and Dynamic Co-ordination*. Oxford, UK: Palgrave Macmillan, which provides a strategic, resource and knowledge accumulation based view of the Indian software industry.
10. Source: various reports.

11. Source: *Dataquest*, 15 July 2006, Vol. XXIV(13).
12. Source: India FDI Fact Sheet, March 2006. Available at *http://dipp. nic.in/fdi_statistics/india_fdi_index.htm*
13. Data based on reports in various newspapers such as *The Economic Times, The Hindu* and *Business Standard*.
14. Source: NASSCOM Strategic Review 2006 – The IT Industry in India.
15. Source: NASSCOM.
16. India has its own patent laws as set forth by the Indian Patent Office.
17. The Indian Patent Laws are also TRIPS compliant.
18. Source: *Dataquest*, 15 July 2006, Vol. XXIV(13).
19. Ibid.

4

China versus India – a SWOT perspective

Introduction

Drawing on the PESTEL analyses of the Chinese and Indian software industries presented in the preceding two chapters, this chapter performs a strengths, weaknesses, opportunities and threats (SWOT) analysis on each country's software industry, and compares and contrasts them in relation to each other as well as North America and Europe. The implications for both China and India will be discussed in Chapter 8, whereas Chapter 9 will discuss specific customer- and market-oriented strategies for China and India.

SWOT analysis of China's software industry

In contrast with India's software industry development, China's software industry has been domestically focused since the beginning. Only recently did the industry start to seriously look into India's success in software exports. Another important differing factor is the different roles played by the government. As indicated in the previous two chapters, the Chinese government has been much more of a force in shaping the trajectory of its software industry compared with India. These two features have significant implications on all the aspects related with the strengths, weaknesses, opportunities and threats of the Chinese software industry.

Strengths

Strong government support

Deng Xiaoping's often-repeated words: 'Science and technology are the chief productive forces' reflect the significance of indigenous mastery of technology to the vision of a modern, powerful economy. China's 10th Five-Year Plan (2001–2005) identifies software as a critical or 'pillar' industry that is essential to economic progress and national security, hence deserving government promotion, along with more established industries such as computer manufacturing, telecommunications, lasers, and aerospace.[1] The current government is even more determined in its aim of developing China into an innovative society. In launching the 'National Medium- and Long-Term Programs for Scientific and Technological Development (2006–2020)', the central government has vowed to spend more on science and technology, and to insist on business reforms. The goal is to move China beyond its dependence on natural resources and cheap labour, and stake its place among the economies that depend on education and information technology. The plan calls for an increase in research and development spending from its current 1.23 per cent of GDP to 2.5 per cent by 2020, putting China in the same range as OECD countries' current scores.[2]

Over the years, China has cultivated a successful domestic hardware industry through state-funded research and development of new technologies, as well as tax incentives. In addition, hardware producers have traditionally bundled software with hardware as part of the total package to be sold on the market. As a result, the software industry in China lags significantly behind world market leaders. China's top leaders have recognised this disparity and have shifted industrial policies in favour of the development of the software industry. China has instigated a number of policies ranging from export incentives to value-added tax rebates and financial assistance for small businesses, as well as laws addressing intellectual property rights protection.

Despite China's membership of the WTO and the creation of policies that encourage investment in the software sector, government authorities have created situations that favour SOEs in some cases. As part of a government contract, a government agency could require companies to obtain a Certification of Capability and Quality that is issued by the Ministry of Information Industry (MII) at the national, provincial, and municipal levels. Whether MII will grant this certificate depends on a firm's total net assets, registered capital, and annual revenues, rather than the ability of the company to complete the work requested. By most accounts, it is very difficult for a private sector company to receive such a certificate based on these standards.[3]

High growth

China's software output has grown at an average annual rate of 30 per cent since 1995 and is predicted to continue this rapid growth for several more years. There are approximately 20 million small- to medium-sized enterprises in China, which provides a substantial business user base. This base is expected to increase the domestic software market from 10 billion to 100 billion RMB in 5 to 8 years. Furthermore, the proportion of the population with personal computers is ever increasing: reaching nearly 29 million on shipments in 2000, and the proportion of telephone users has rapidly increased, reaching 145 million users in 2000, of which 85.2 million were mobile users.[4] All of these will spur the demand for software.

Strong supporting and related industries

The industry will have a great potential to grow: it is located in the world's fastest growing market alongside a dynamic IT manufacturing sector. Some aspects of the Chinese economy are expected to have a positive influence on the industry's growth, such as the strong manufacturing sector, which uses software in many products even beyond computer equipment, e.g. telecommunications equipment (some of which is now 50 per cent software), consumer electronics products, automobile machinery etc.

Weaknesses

Although China's software industry has achieved some degree of success and shows huge long-term potential, there are still some major problems that are becoming obstacles in the path of China's software industry development. The first problem is that the massive issue of software piracy is not well under control. The Business Software Alliance estimates that pirated software accounts for 92 per cent of the Chinese software market – the second highest piracy rate among the 86 countries it tracks. The same study values lost revenue due to piracy in China at $2.4 billion. While the amount of the loss may be overestimated considering most pirate copy purchasers would not have spent much more to own an authentic program, it definitely impacts the incentive for both foreign and domestic software firms to innovate and market their software products in China. According to a survey conducted by People's Daily in 2001, more than a quarter of Chinese software firms believe software piracy is the most important barrier to their development, and approximately one-fifth of the companies complain that software piracy has seriously constrained further R&D investments into software products.

Recognising the negative impact of piracy on the software market, the Chinese government has taken actions to fight against the production and sale of pirated software. Many agree that it is an uphill battle that has to overcome many obstacles. For example, software piracy is so prevalent that it has become a habit, even for consumers who can afford legitimate copies, to purchase bootleg copies. However, how to effectively control software piracy is still a major challenge to China.

The second problem is that the majority of Chinese software firms lack competence in the software market. This problem can be identified from two aspects:

- Chinese players in the high end of the software market. China's domestic software industry is still at a primitive stage of development, and few Chinese software companies, if any, are capable of developing upper-level software, such as operating systems. In 2002, 85 per cent of China's software products and services were in the categories of maintenance and applications, and the market share of system software is negligible. Application software represents 64.5 per cent of the total revenue, implying the revenue from system software still contributes less to the overall revenue. In fact, the most valued market segments such as operating systems and major packaged software are dominated by foreign software superpowers.

- Fragmentation: the scale of Chinese software firms is generally too small. China's software industry is an extremely fragmented industry consisting of thousands of small, undercapitalised firms with few competitive advantages relative to the foreign corporations that dominate the market. The size of software firms matters in the market because a firm's economic scale predetermines its ability to compete and to survive. According to the MII and National Bureau of Statistics (NBS) of China, by 2002 China had 4,700 software companies, approximately double that of a year previously. However, China's software companies are still relatively small. In 2002, two thirds of

Chinese software companies had a number of employees not exceeding 50. Approximately 26 per cent of the companies had between 50–300 employees. The revenue for 95.5 per cent of Chinese software companies was less than US$12 million (RMB 100 million) in 2002.

Furthermore, Chinese software companies lack senior professionals in core technology competencies. In 2002, of 59,000 software personnel, 7 per cent had Masters degrees, 33 per cent had Bachelors degrees, and 17 per cent had polytechnic degrees, and there were only 157,000 research and development professionals scattered among 4,700 companies.

By the end of 2002, the number of Chinese software companies certified by the Capability Maturity Model Integration Certification (CMMI; *http://www.sei.cmu.edu/*), an internationally-recognised standard of quality management for software firms, was only 2.5 per cent as a global proportion. Of the five levels of CMM standards, only a few Chinese firms have reached the middle level – CMM3 – so far, and none have attained a level higher than that.

The low competency of Chinese software companies overall has become the bottleneck of China's software industry development. One of the direct outcomes is that it is hard for Chinese companies to compete effectively in the international outsourcing market, in which India software companies have won majority of the contracts. In 2002 the revenue of China's software industry (US$13.3 billion) was about the same level as that of India (US$ 12 billion). However, China's revenue from software export in 2002, at US$1.5 billion, was far below that of India ($9.5 billion).

In the domestic software market, Chinese software companies have been facing more pressure from powerful foreign competitors. Foreign software companies in China's market are normally more competitive and more experienced, particularly when they have monopoly power in the software market. The competition between Kingsoft and Microsoft's Chinese word processing software is a classic case. Kingsoft's Chinese processing system had a market share of approximately 90 per cent in 1994. But it hit rock bottom due to competition from the Microsoft Word system. With its advantages in operating systems, Microsoft launched its Windows XP software that undermined Kingsoft's efforts with its WPS Word processing system. Finally, Kingsoft released WPS Office 2002, the latest version of its word-processing system, to contend with its powerful US rival Microsoft's Office XP. Still, Microsoft is now believed to have approximately 90 per cent of the Chinese market for word processing software.

Ironically the overzealous support from the government may become a weakness for the healthy development of China's software industry. As noted by Saxenian, 'The shift to market-coordination thus coexists with the aggressive promotion and preferential treatment – either explicit or implicit – of domestic producers or national "champions".' 'Moreover the identification and promotion of select producers, by providing government contracts, preferential access to capital, and regulatory priority, leaves open a multiplicity of opportunities for bureaucratic discretion and corruption.'[5]

On the micro level, there are some inherited weaknesses in China's software firms. The lack of managerial experience and models for software development is one of the most significant weaknesses of China's software industry.[6] The Chinese software firms' process capabilities are believed to be poorer than India's. Poor process capabilities were cited by Huawei, a large Chinese firm, as a reason why it located a major software development facility in Bangalore, India.[7]

Shortage of funding is a major obstacle to China's software industry development. There is a strong bias among banks in China against lending to private enterprises because it is far more risky than investing in state-owned enterprises. This problem is particularly acute in software because the banks have virtually no credit analysis capabilities, and in any case prefer to invest in businesses with physical (as opposed to intangible, intellectual) assets. Venture capital (VC) has been an important mechanism for financing new technology ventures in a mature market economy, but it is not an option to most Chinese software firms at this stage as the VC industry is still in its infancy. As a result, the great majority of software enterprises in China are self-financed. This is one of the reasons why many large software firms in China are affiliates of large IT manufacturing or telecoms firms. This issue will be analysed further in Chapter 6, on interrelationships and horizontal strategies.

With the deepening of multinational corporations' presence in China, the industry has witnessed increasing capital investment of these corporations in Chinese software firms that will help alleviate the funding problem. For example, Intel announced in June 2006 that it would fund four more IT companies, bringing to 12 the number of investments made from its $200 million China Technology Fund that was launched a year previously. The latest investments are in a semiconductor-design company, two software developers, and a company that specialises in marketing on university campuses. Since starting to invest in China in 1998, Intel has invested in nearly 60 companies based in or focused on China up to 2006.[8]

Opportunities

Opportunities from government-initiated projects[9]

Four key factors are opening up significant opportunities for IT hardware and software suppliers to take advantage of China's vast consumer market. These are: (1) the government's informatisation drive, as stated in its Tenth Five-Year Plan, to spread the use of information technologies among communities, government agencies, and China's traditional industries; (2) the 'Go West' campaign to narrow the digital divide between Eastern and Western China and other similar projects to reduce regional imbalance in economic development; (3) China's accession to the WTO; and (4) the 2008 Beijing Olympic Games and its particular focus on high-tech applications.

According to IDC, China's increase in e-government spending of nearly 40 per cent annually between 2001 and 2003 provides IT firms with the opportunity to introduce solutions that will help the national, provincial, and municipal governments offer online services to their citizens. These solutions include networking hardware and software, Chinese language database software, Chinese language content management tools, portal software, and network security solutions. Thanks to the opening of markets resulting from China's membership of the WTO, foreign IT suppliers will have new business prospects in traditional industries, such as manufacturing and banking, that need to upgrade their systems to become competitive internationally. These industries will require solutions (e.g. enterprise resource planning, customer relationship management, and supply chain management packages) that will help them become more efficient in delivering products to customers and receiving inputs from their suppliers. IT companies should take advantage of China's rapidly-growing market for IT services by not only targeting the traditional industries, but also by assisting state-owned enterprises to increase their competitiveness through selecting the right combination of equipment and software.

The imbalance between the stages of economic development among China's different regions means a great long-term opportunity for the software industry. One negative outcome of the two decades of economic development has been the expanding disparity among different regions, which to a large extent was the result of the central government's skewed policy. In the 1980s the southeast region of China became the early success story in China's economic reform due to its geographic proximity to Hong Kong. Shanghai became the beneficiary of the government's favourable policy in 1990s. In order to reduce the imbalance among different regions, recently the government has proposed massive projects for developing the west, revitalising the traditionally heavy-industry based north-eastern region, and the most recent move of making the regions surrounding Beijing the hottest zone of economic reform. With each region emulating the experiences of earlier prosperous regions, new demands for software products and services are created.

IT suppliers should benefit from the $24 million investment that China's Ministry of Science and Technology is making available to bridge the country's digital divide through the wide variety of programs that are a part of the 'Go West' initiative. IT solutions companies will be needed to educate communities, local governments, and businesses in Western China in various uses of information technology and to train citizens on how to use computers and the Internet. Because of the large rural economy in this region, US software firms will find substantial demand for Chinese-language software targeted at the agricultural sector and packages that would help farmers distribute their products more efficiently throughout China. In addition, US Internet content providers will have an opportunity to develop Chinese-language content to increase the use of the Internet, especially for educational purposes in schools and hospitals, in Western China.

China's successful bid for the 2008 Olympics, to be held in Beijing, will present domestic and foreign IT companies with enormous opportunities to sell their equipment, software, and services. The IT projects envisioned by the municipal government of Beijing will require a wide range of products such as smart card technologies, broadband applications, database applications, e-commerce platforms, network security solutions, simulation software, games software relating to Olympic sports, and voice recognition software.

Foreign suppliers interested in pursuing opportunities in China's ICT markets should recognise the differences in business and cultural styles between their home countries and China and develop an appropriate market entry strategy. Some form of local presence is essential. Options include using agents and distributors; partnering with large IT firms, systems integrators, or consultants; partnering with like-minded Chinese small and medium-sized enterprises (SMEs) with complimentary skills or products; or setting up a local office staffed by local employees to do marketing and training and to provide ongoing support. Even though China is a very large market of 1.3 billion people, it is essential that businesses understand consumer behaviour in the provinces/regions they are targeting. For example, spending patterns and needs of ICT end-users in the Pearl River Delta region are very different from those of end-users in the Yangtze River Delta region and from those in Western China.

Opportunities from the Chinese Diaspora: learning from the experience of India

Since the initial wave of students and emigrant IT workers from China going to study and work in the US was approximately one or two decades behind that of India, it is believed that in the near future the return of Chinese citizens from abroad will play an important role in the opening of international software products and services markets for Chinese firms.

Opportunities in related and supporting industries

In the telecommunications area, the build-out of 3G wireless networks will offer opportunities not only for telecommunications equipment vendors, but also for companies supplying a wide range of associated software applications, including roaming, billing, and user application packages. China's accession to the WTO has opened new opportunities for foreign telecommunications service providers to invest in a Chinese market that had previously been closed to foreign participation.

In the area of e-commerce, China's business-to-business market should continue to offer IT firms the best prospects for exports. Demand for web developers, web hosting services providers, and e-commerce consultants is particularly high. E-commerce products and services localised for the Chinese users should enjoy the most success.

Threats

Piracy is a major threat to the development of the software industry

According to the Business Software Alliance's June 2002 piracy study, China had a 92 per cent business software piracy rate in 2001, accounting for nearly $1.7 billion in retail software revenue losses due to copyright violations. Although the piracy rate did decrease two percentage points from 2000, the dollar value of losses increased by over $500 million. Since 1996, China has not been able to reduce its piracy rate to below 90 per cent. It had the second-highest piracy rate in the Asia-Pacific region, which averaged 54 per cent in 2001, and accounted for 35 per cent of the revenue losses in the region due to piracy. In comparison to other parts of the world with strong software markets, such as North America and Western Europe, where the piracy rates in 2001 averaged 26 per cent and 37 per cent, respectively, China needs to strengthen its intellectual property rights protection laws and enforcement mechanisms at the national, provincial, and municipal levels significantly to develop a domestic software industry and compete internationally.

The largest obstacle to deterring piracy in China is corporate end-user piracy. While PC prices have declined significantly over the years, packaged software prices have not. Using pirated versions of applications software sold on the black market for a fraction of the cost of the legal licensed version is a regular practice among most businesses. The Computer Software Protection Regulations define rights and obligations of computer software use but do not explicitly prohibit software piracy. Copyright authorities at the local level are usually small offices, making enforcement quite difficult. China's accession to the WTO and sign-up to the TRIPS agreement will pressure China to become more aggressive in enforcing its intellectual property rights protection laws.

Threat from human capital shortage

The shortage of highly-skilled software professionals is a concern for many software companies in China and poses a long-term threat to the industry development. In 2003 there were approximately 4 billion IT personnel working in the IT industry, including 590,000 in the software sector. According to an estimation by the MII, the shortage in the software industry is approximately 150,000. Approximately 37,000 students graduate annually from Chinese universities and colleges with computer science degrees; 50 per cent have a software certificate and only approximately 5 per cent have advanced (masters or doctorate) degrees.[10] Many industry insiders believe that solving the problem of a lack of high-end talent is the most urgent need for the Chinese software industry. One reason is that high-end software program managers prefer to work for the multinationals that can afford to pay higher wages and provide better training and career development paths.

The brain drain problem is also a major threat to China's software industry development. It is estimated that 30 per cent of the computer science degree earners from China's most elite universities went abroad to pursue higher degrees in the 1990s, and the return rate is very low. In contrast, Indian Diasporas from the US have played a critical role in the success of Indian software exports. They transfer not only technology and capital, but also managerial and institutional know-how. More importantly, they link local firms directly with markets and networks abroad. However, there is evidence that the number of returning Chinese students who have studied and worked abroad is increasing rapidly. In the long term, these returnees will be important for the Chinese software industry to close the gap with India and more advanced countries.

Threats from foreign companies

Amid the dominance of the multinationals in China's packaged software products, the development of China's software products market segment seems to be a daunting task. As for the nascent software service industry, which is mainly targeting the Japanese market, it is also facing challenges from India that has a great deal of sophisticated experience and a successful track record in this area. Transforming these threatening competitors into cooperative partners would be the correct approach for the Chinese software industry to enhance its capability and move up the value chain.

SWOT analysis of India's software industry

Ever since its early stages, India's software industry has grown steadily, and has been the subject of many studies and analyses. This section presents a SWOT perspective of the Indian software industry, analysing its strengths, weaknesses, opportunities and threats, and comparing and contrasting them with the Chinese software industry as well as with the North American and European software industries. The SWOT analysis is presented along four major themes, namely industry capability and capacity, business environment and ecosystem, institutional framework, and industry competitiveness.

It must be emphasised that this SWOT analysis should be viewed in the perspective of the characteristics of the Indian software industry, which, at least to date, has largely been a service-intensive and export-oriented industry. Although the structure of the Indian software industry

Table 4.1	SWOT analysis of the Indian software industry

Strengths	Weaknesses
■ Large, well-qualified, young, and English-proficient resource base (large scale) ■ Strong operational capability and quality processes focus ■ Attractive cost structures ■ Versatile technical and technology skill base ■ Established global delivery model ■ Favourable government policies ■ Strong management experience ■ Multi-country development footprint ■ Customer relationship capital ■ Multiplicity of business models and associated delivery capability ■ Growing domain skills ■ Substantial presence of MNCs ■ Social networks and entrepreneurial growth; strong network with Silicon Valley ■ Work ethics and committed labour force ■ Good image of the industry; preference for software jobs ■ Established brand and global reputation	■ Meagre intellectual property reservoir ■ Barriers due to low domain skills ■ Inadequate skills for large/complex/integrated program/project management ■ Overdependence on the US market ■ Poor physical infrastructure ■ Workforce attrition leading to knowledge loss ■ Eroding cost advantage due to rising wages ■ Perception of political instability and other geo-political risks due to cross-border tension ■ IPR enforcement and inefficient legal system (when compared to North America and Europe, but better than China) ■ Foreign exchange fluctuations ■ Bureaucracy and corruption ■ Relatively inflexible labour laws ■ Burdensome taxation rules ■ Poor industry-academia linkage
Opportunities	**Threats**
■ Growing cost consciousness resulting in increased offshoring ■ Growing global IT spend ■ Large, multi-year outsourcing deals ■ Opportunities in other geographies and verticals ■ High-end consulting and business solutions, capitalising on the growing domain skills ■ Growing domestic market ■ R&D outsourcing and engineering services ■ Harness partnership and alliances ■ Scale through globalisation and inorganic growth ■ R&D-based differentiation ■ Emerging product innovation	■ Competition from other emerging offshore destinations (low-cost economies) ■ Increasing margin pressure ■ Commoditisation of traditional application development and maintenance services ■ Emerging delivery paradigms such a utility computing and software as service ■ Failure to discover vectors of differentiation ■ Growing public and labour union resistance to offshoring ■ Talent availability not in synch with growth ■ Growing MNC presence ■ Changes in immigration regulations ■ Adoption of the offshoring model by global IT firms

resembles that of the Chinese software industry to some extent, there are significant differences when compared to the software industries in North America and Central Europe.

Firstly, in India, the software industry has developed and grown irrespective of the domestic demand. Secondly, by and large, the Indian software industry has been a service-providing industry, supplying software or programming talent to corporations in North America, Europe and Japan. In contrast, the software industries in North America and Europe have grown rather holistically in response to domestic demands and the needs of other industrial sectors, and have included both products and services. The Chinese software industry, by contrast, developed with a domestic focus and it is only recently that China has discovered the huge potential of software service exports. In addition, it is important to recognise that the Indian software industry includes not only those firms that are incorporated in India but also subsidiaries of foreign firms.

Table 4.1 below captures the strengths, weaknesses, opportunities and threats for the Indian software industry.

Strengths

India's prominence on the global software industry landscape can be largely attributed to a vast, high-quality, English speaking, youthful talent pool. The availability of the talent pool continues to be a favourable factor for the Indian software industry as it allows achievements of scale. China also has a large talent pool, and the Chinese government has taken upon itself to increase the size and the quality of that talent pool. However, there are two important ways in which the Indian software industry currently has the upper hand. First and foremost, India not only has a large, high-quality talent pool, but also its human capital is quite experienced compared to that of China. Secondly, India has a much younger talent pool when compared to that of China,[11] which is also faced with a rapidly aging population. Moreover, the aggressive government focus in China on rapidly expanding the resource base has an implication on the quality of the resource. Europe and North America, on the other hand, have good quality talent but do not have the scale needed to compete in the resource-intensive software and IT services businesses.

When compared to India, the Chinese software industry suffers from the fact that it is highly fragmented, with many thousands of small players. Indian software companies are significantly greater in size, both in terms of their annual revenue and manpower base. For example, the top five Indian firms each have revenues in excess of US $1 billion and employ more than 40,000 people each. There is no single Chinese company that is anywhere near these Indian firms in terms of size. Many Indian firms are also listed in overseas stock exchanges such as NASDAQ, NYSE and LSE, and enjoy a high market cap.

Of course, lower cost structures that have so far been responsible for fuelling industry growth continue to be attractive when compared to North America and Central Europe. Currently, the average cost per software professional in India is lower by roughly 15 per cent compared to an equivalent professional in China, and almost 1/8th of an equivalent professional in North America and Central Europe.[12] The software firms in India have adopted and evolved best practices in human resource management and invested considerably in employee attraction, development and retention, as well as instituting attractive ESOP programmes. The Chinese software firms seem to be considerably behind on this front.

Alongside the inherent strengths such as a large talent pool and lower cost structures, the Indian software industry derives its strengths from capability build-up that has happened over a period of time. In fact, the operational capability the Indian software firms have developed over the years through perpetual refinement is not easy to replicate. For example, the collective management experience that the Indian software industry has acquired over two decades is quite substantial. This is particularly true for the competencies and processes related to management of globally-distributed knowledge work. The global delivery model, pioneered by the Indian software industry, has been refined over a period of time, which means that the Indian software firms have learned to optimise the various elements that constitute the global delivery model's supply chain. Optimising the global delivery value chain also meant investments in processes, methods and tools, which is shown by the industry's demonstrated excellence in software quality. Moreover, the Indian software industry has also learned to profitably operate through a range of business models such as time and material, fixed price contracts, build-operate-transfer, ODC (offshore development centre), and risk-reward, which means that the industry has developed the managerial, organisational and process capabilities corresponding to each of these. The Chinese as well as the North American and European software industries do not match up to India's management and software delivery capability, size and organisational maturity, especially as it relates to delivering in a globally distributed work environment through a range of business models supported by high process maturity.

The Indian software industry possesses a wide spectrum of technical skills, ranging from mainframe technology to Internet technology, covering a broad array of operating systems (Unix, Windows, Linux), platforms (.NET and J2EE), and development environments and tools, in addition to intensive knowledge of software engineering techniques and processes as testified by their maturity levels on the SW-CMM model. Over a period of time, as the industry has catered to diverse verticals such as banking and finance, retail, transportation, manufacturing, etc., there has been an accumulation of the vital domain knowledge, which is allowing the industry to approach their clients with better value propositions. The software industry in China does not yet have such a broad technology skill base, software engineering process maturity or domain knowledge, whereas in North America and Europe, while broad-ranging technical skills and domain expertise are surely available, they fall short in the areas of software engineering and quality processes when compared to the Indian software industry.

The Indian software industry has also rapidly expanded its footprint into many countries, establishing sales offices and delivery centres to cater to customers and markets in an effective manner. Many leading Indian software companies such as Tata Consultancy Services, Infosys Technologies, Wipro Technologies and Satyam Computer Services have globalised their development operations in other low-cost countries, achieving a multi-country development footprint. Interestingly, all these companies have established development centres in China and are rapidly expanding their bases there. The same is generally not true for the Chinese software industry, except for a few rare exceptions such as Huawei Technologies and TCL that have established development operations in India. The North American and European MNCs, however, have a global footprint anyway.

The Indian software industry also draws its strength from the valuable relationship and social capital it has accumulated over the years of its existence. Specifically, the industry enjoys substantial relationship capital with its customers by virtue of years of work with them, which, in turn, results in a lock-in effect. This is evident in the fact that all leading Indian software services vendors derive nearly 50–80 per cent of annual revenues come from repeat business from existing customers. The Chinese software industry does not yet enjoy such relationship capital and, given that it is a fragmented industry, it will be a while before it can acquire such strength on this front. In addition, the Chinese software industry has primarily grown in response to the domestic market so lacks the skills required to work with diverse cultures and handle customer idiosyncrasies, something that the Indian software industry is dexterous at. The North American and European software industries, especially in the software and IT services sector, do have the relationship capital but do not match India's skills in managing diverse customer idiosyncrasies and cultural contexts.

The Indian Diaspora has been instrumental in the formation of social networks that result in accumulation of valuable social capital and promotion of entrepreneurship. This is particularly true of strong social ties with the entrepreneurial ecosystem in Silicon Valley, which not only catalysed the inflow of venture capital but also expanded the realm of offshore technology work by locating R&D activities in India. The Chinese software industry has near-equal advantage of such social ties in that the large Chinese community residing in the US, as well as their movement back home, provides venture capital inflow along with influencing substantial FDI.

The economic reform process set in motion in India in 1991, which resulted in a series of important policy measures, continues to benefit the industry and also attract foreign direct investment in the software and IT sector. In fact, in every Union Budget the government has instituted progressive policy measures and incentives to promote the software industry, catalysing industry growth and competitiveness. Additionally, the government's moves to open up the telecoms sector have been instrumental in catalysing the growth in the software and IT services sector. A strong banking and financial sector and a vibrant capital market lend further strength to the Indian software industry. The Chinese government has also instituted a number of policy measures to promote the software industry and software exports, and has done so rather aggressively. In fact, in the case of India, the government's role can be described as facilitative at best, whereas the Chinese government has acted as a partner for the country's software industry. In comparison, the federal policies in North America and Europe have traditionally been progressive and well-rounded, and so there has not been any exclusive promotion of the software industry except for a recent organised thrust within the European Union to gain strengths in ICT.

India's strength comes from the constituents of its workforce that are committed, flexible, and effective in handling diversity and working with other cultures. This strength is augmented by a large number of job applicants who pursue careers in the software industry because of its image and prospects. This is also true in the case of the Chinese software industry except that it does not yet have the size, management skills, and broad-ranging technical skills that the companies in the Indian software industry enjoy. The flexibility and the continued focus on learning that characterises the Indian software industry give it an edge when compared to North America and Europe, that are thought to have a relatively inflexible workforce both in terms of adapting to the demands of global work and demonstrating agility to embrace new technical developments.

Finally, strong corporate governance in the Indian software companies works to their advantage because it instils client and investor confidence and trust, resulting in business growth. In contrast, numerous reports suggest opaque corporate governance in Chinese software companies.

Weaknesses

The very software services business that raised India into the limelight and is the source of its growing export revenues also has inherent weaknesses, some of which could be detrimental in the long run for the industry as a whole. First and foremost, the Indian software industry has very little intellectual property (IP) that it can leverage in the wake of growing global competition. Traditionally, providing software services to customers did not really require focus on R&D and intellectual property generation, except as necessitated for improving the delivery capability.

In recent times, however, there has been a sign of a growing IP and patent culture, although it is difficult to establish that these companies have achieved marketplace leverage due their IP assets. In the financial year 2005–2006, the combined patent filing by Indian software companies (MNC subsidiaries excluded) was less than 50.[13] The legal framework in India is strong, but resolution of disputes takes a long time. Moreover, the enforcement of intellectual property rights is also still weak compared to North America and Europe. For example, during 2005–2006 an estimated US $600 million to US $1 billion worth of revenue loss was incurred due to piracy of software products and packages. So, it appears that the inefficient legal environment also has been responsible for the low IPR reservoir within the Indian software industry. The North American as well as European software industries score very highly on matters related to intellectual property, both in terms of innovation propensity and a strong legal environment, although like India, the European Union does not recognise software and business method patents. The Chinese software industry, however, suffers from a weak legal environment and rampant IP violation, both of which have been a cause for serious concern for foreign firms.

The absence of a domestic market has also been responsible for an almost non-existent focus on the creation of intellectual property. Moreover, the industry–academia linkage, which is a potential source for fuelling the creation of intellectual property creation, has been rather abysmal, and there is no sign of this improving. By contrast, the Chinese software industry has had, and continues to have, a strong domestic market, and this is also the case with the North American and European software industries. China also has access to a large manufacturing base, which provides additional revenue opportunities for the local software industry. The software industries in North America and Europe benefit from a strong industry–academia interaction, and increasingly this is the case with the Chinese software industry as well.

With the emergence of other low-cost countries on the software services scene, as well as overall intensification of competition, the need for differentiation has become pronounced. The industry has long since talked about 'moving up the value chain', but the actual industry growth is seen in further low-value work such as IT-enabled services and business process outsourcing work. Even today, the revenue composition of the Indian software industry suggests that largely software and IT services are being provided, comprised of low-value work such as software programming and maintenance services, and a host of IT-enabled services. The growth of knowledge process outsourcing (KPO) businesses in areas such as financial equity research and patent searching and drafting is encouraging though because of the high skill levels involved, but these are very labour-intensive activities and could be constrained by a lack of suitable manpower.

Moving up the value chain has been recognised as a competitive necessity for the further growth and competitiveness of the Indian software industry. However, a lack of in-depth domain skills and the ability to manage complex, integrated programs have been major barriers to value migration. While these problems are more severe for the Chinese software industry, the North American and to some extent the European software industries have the upper hand here.

Another noticeable weakness of the Indian software industry stems from its over-dependence on the US market,[14] which means that business cycles in the US have a direct impact on the Indian software industry. This also means that the industry's overall learning has been aligned to the US markets and culture, leaving the industry so attuned to the customer idiosyncrasies there that it needs to develop the acumen to effectively handle other geographies. This is by and large not the case for the Chinese software industry, which generates most of its revenues from the domestic market and exports are spread across USA, Japan and Korea. Neither is this an issue for the North American and European software industries that have a well-rounded domestic as well as global market presence.

The cost competitiveness of the Indian software industry, which has been a key factor in propelling the growth of the industry, is gradually eroding owing to wage inflation. Even though currently the average cost per software engineer in India is approximately 1/8th of that of an equivalent professional in the US or Central Europe, and approximately 15 per cent less when compared to an equivalent Chinese software professional, the industry will need to contain its operational costs in order to continue to be attractive. Currently, however, India has a distinct advantage as far as its cost competitiveness is concerned, especially when viewed in the light of the value it offers.

Another major weakness of the Indian software industry pertains to the high attrition rate of 15–30 per cent that it faces, although a similar trend has been seen in other regions such as Silicon Valley at the time of the dot-com job boom of 1996–2001. However, employee movement results in knowledge loss and prevents the collective build-up of much-needed domain skills, besides the need for re-investing in training and learning. Many customers attribute their unwillingness to send high-value work to India to a high employee turnover. Various reports indicate that this is indeed the situation in the Chinese software industry as well, where attrition is at an average of 20 per cent, which is a cause for serious concern because of the limited base of experienced resources. The North American and European software industries do not face such high employee turnover, although it must also be recognised that the rate of employee turnover is also a function of the available opportunities and growth prospects in a given industry.

The most burning weakness currently, however, is country's buckling infrastructure, especially in the cities where most software companies are located. Poor airport infrastructures, road connectivity, communication infrastructures and power supply situations are not only directly impacting productivity (due to long commute times to work) and high operating costs, but are also affecting investment decisions in favour of other countries. China scores very highly when it comes to physical infrastructure, which is on par with the US and developed countries in Europe.

The software industry in India also suffers from other weaknesses as well, some of them real and some perceived. For example, the exports-intensive software industry suffers from foreign exchange fluctuations, and in this respect a large dependence on the US market is problematic. The Chinese software industry is not free from this problem either, and is amenable to shocks that arise from valuation of the Yuan. The level of bureaucracy and corruption that the businesses in India encounter is still high. China, on the other hand, has perhaps a less-bureaucratic business environment but corruption is high there as well. These, for example, are not issues the North American and European software industries encounter. Likewise, the Indian labour laws are considered to be rigid when compared to China or North America, but are surely more flexible compared to European countries. The taxation rules in India are also considered burdensome by Western companies. Additionally, although the perception of cross-border tensions posing a geo-political risk to businesses is not so real, it leads to foreign companies controlling or diverting their investments to other countries or distributing investments across geographies. This applies to China as well, which also has ongoing tensions with North Korea and faces a looming uncertainty over Taiwan's future.

Opportunities

The Indian software industry has gradually upgraded itself to handle larger, more sophisticated outsourcing deals. Today, all large Indian IT consulting and software services firms are competing for multi-billion, multi-year outsourcing deals, and in recent times there have been a number of success stories of Indian firms being awarded portions of such large deals. Unlike previously, today the companies outsourcing their software and IT work find they have more choices and prefer to divide the total outsourcing deal among various vendors to get the best cost–value proposition and to minimise risks as well as vendor opportunism. The Indian software and IT service companies, because of their predictable, high-quality delivery and low-cost structures, are increasingly receiving a significant portion of large outsourcing deals, especially for application development and maintenance.

During 2006–2008, an estimated US $100 billion worth of outsourcing contracts will be up for renewal,[15] which points to a substantial business opportunity that lies ahead for the Indian software industry. Moreover, the Indian software and IT services industry also has the opportunity to provide integrated offshore outsourcing services by bringing together disparate services such as application development and maintenance, business process outsourcing and remote infrastructure management services. This not only allows the construction of a better value proposition to clients, but also facilitates a synergistic leverage of knowledge and skills across activities. Although, the participants from the North American and European software industries are well-equipped to pursue such large, high-value opportunities, their cost structures could be a hindrance to their competitiveness. The Chinese software industry, especially when viewed in the context of the exports or outsourcing market, does not currently have the scale, capability or credentials to generate confidence among the prospective clients to undertake such contracts.

The global software and IT industry, growing at an annual rate of 7 per cent[16] is replete with opportunities, and the Indian software industry is in a strong position to capitalise on these opportunities by leveraging its learning, capability and reputation. To start with, a growing cost consciousness among enterprises globally is expected to accelerate the pace of offshoring, and India, with its cumulative knowledge base in performing offshore work and its proven capabilities, stands to gain from this trend. Coupled with the intensification of offshoring, a rising global IT spend makes the opportunities for the Indian software industry more compelling. The Chinese software industry also surely stands to gain from this trend, whereas forecasts suggest that the North American and European software industries will be negatively impacted, except perhaps in some Eastern European countries.

The Indian software industry also has huge opportunities in the consulting space, and many Indian firms are now systematically addressing this area. All large Indian software and IT companies now have dedicated consulting organisations, and being a late entrant into the consulting space they have the advantage of learning from the mistakes and shortcomings of the incumbents, and can redefine the way consulting value deliverance is managed. Infosys Technologies, for example, set up a wholly-owned consulting subsidiary, incorporated in the US, called Infosys Consulting.

There is also a significant market for providing technology-based business solutions. For example, as a consequence of what emerging technologies such as RFID, enterprise mobility, web services and service-oriented architecture, grid computing, etc. offer for business competitiveness, a whole new and lucrative business solutions market has spawned. Many Indian firms are actively pursuing solutions sales to capture the high-margin business opportunities this segment offers and, in effect, are seeking to become partners in business transformation. The domain skills that the Indian firms acquired over the years in working with diverse set of clients in various verticals is proving to be helpful in defining and developing business solutions. However, whether it is consulting, domain skills or emerging technologies-based business solutions, the North American and European software industries have the upper hand over the Indian software industry, whereas the Chinese software industry is still not in a competitive position in these regards. The North American and European firms in particular are in a unique position to leverage their relationship capital and years of experience in consulting with clients across various domains, and ensure their competitive positioning despite higher prices.

There is also a huge market for product development outsourcing and engineering services, and various forecasts suggest that this segment will grow to a US $150 billion global market by 2009. Indian firms have already begun to systematically address this market segment, deriving US $4.7 billion in revenues during the financial year ended March 2006[17] and treating this segment as a strategic growth opportunity. Increasingly, technology companies are finding outsourcing to be an effective mechanism to optimise their investments and to cope with rising technological and market uncertainties. In addition, the growing markets in India and other emerging economies in the Asia-Pacific region also present significant product localisation and system integration opportunities for Indian software firms. Like India, the Chinese software industry also stands to gain, especially through localisation work and because of its significant manufacturing base, but it appears that the major portion of the work will be heading in India's direction because of its strong engineering skills base and proven capability.

Many Indian software firms have partnerships or alliances with leading software companies such as IBM, Microsoft, Oracle and SAP, but so far these partnerships have by and large focused on competency enablement in their respective technologies and platforms primarily aimed at facilitating systems integration. There is clearly an opportunity for Indian software firms to leverage their relationships with leading software product vendors to pursue joint deals, developing and selling solutions jointly, and expanding their respective market outreach. Obviously, such partnership pursuits will equally benefit the North American and European software industries. The Chinese software companies are also in a good position to leverage such partnerships to cater to local and neighbouring markets, although they may be limited by their current capabilities. Additionally, the area of open source software support offers good business opportunities for software firms in India, especially in the wake of the growing adoption of open source software, and the Chinese software firms have equal access to this opportunity, although the overall experience and skills base within the Indian software industry gives its players an upper hand here.

The opportunity to strengthen their foothold in the global marketplace by scaling up through globalisation and growing inorganically through acquisitions is also ripe for the players in the Indian software industry. Many Indian companies already have software development and delivery operations in the USA, Canada, Mexico, Brazil, China, Australia and Czech Republic, although they use each location differently with varying capacities. Several Indian firms have also been active on the acquisitions front, seeking to achieve inorganic growth and acquire domain skills and customers. Key examples include acquisition of Expert Systems (Australia) by Infosys Technologies; Nerve Wire (USA), cMango (USA) and Saraware (Finland) by Wipro Technologies; and Azure Solutions (UK) by Subex Systems.[18] The Chinese software industry is far behind on this count, whereas for the North American and European software industries globalisation and acquisitions have always been an integral part of their business strategies.

As it is expected that the software industry will consolidate over the next 5–8 years, the Indian software firms have an opportunity to embrace globalisation to propel their competitiveness. Such globalisation-led growth will also ensure that customers that the Indian software industry caters to will get better value for their money because of physical and cultural proximity, although to achieve predictable, consistent and high-maturity processes across global locations will not be an easy challenge to address.

The Indian software firms have traditionally focused on the US market but other geographies such as EMEA (Europe, Middle East and Africa), Asia Pacific (including Japan and China) and Australia also offer huge market opportunities that Indian firms can tap into. Likewise, other verticals such as healthcare, the aerospace and automotive industries and distribution and logistics, and horizontal areas such as regulatory compliance and security and privacy, present additional growth opportunities. The Chinese software industry will offer tough competition to the Indian software firms in their quest to penetrate the Japanese and Korean markets, although the deteriorating diplomatic relationship between China and Japan could turn things in favour of the Indian software industry and facilitate its access to the large Japanese market.

The domestic market for software and IT services is also growing in India, in line with the overall buoyant growth within the country. Sectors such as banking and finance, retail, energy and infrastructure, telecoms, bioinformatics, etc. are displaying a phenomenal growth as the overall economy is booming and also attracting FDI and venture capital funding. This vast and growing domestic market will undoubtedly generate huge demand for the Indian software industry, much as it is the case for the Chinese software industry, which is operating in the midst of a booming economy and growing domestic market. Typically, the major domestic software projects are very large and complex and, besides a significant commercial appeal, these projects also provide the opportunity to acquire valuable domain and program-management skills. The domestic market also presents an opportunity to develop innovative products with a potential to appeal to global markets. Such products, aligned to the local context (and constraints) of an emerging market like India, have the potential to appeal to global markets as they are likely to be innovations of the disruptive type. Many MNCs have focused part of their R&D budgets in exploring such emerging product market opportunities. There is also a huge opportunity available in the fast growing SME segment, which so far has not been tapped by the Indian software industry.

The Indian software companies are also investing in R&D not only to address the potential domestic market opportunities, but as part of their overall strategy for technological upgradation and value migration to tap into the lucrative consulting and business solutions markets. Drawing from their operational experience and acquired capabilities, many software firms are expanding their service footprints in such areas as bioinformatics, which also offer huge market opportunities. The North American and European software industries have traditionally had a strong R&D focus, but they don't seem to demonstrate a diversification strategy like that of the Indian software industry. The Chinese software industry, by contrast, does not currently show any significant trend towards R&D and certainly not towards diversification or migration from low-level work, although its linkages with academia are strong. However, compared to India, the per annum PhD output in science and engineering is high in China, which could give it an edge from the R&D perspective in the years ahead.

Threats

Interestingly, while the evidence suggests that offshoring is increasingly becoming the norm, there is a clear indication that it is also becoming extremely competitive. In particular, large multi-year outsourcing deals often come with lower margins and with many Indian firms now vying for such large outsourcing deals, their own track record of posting impressive operating margins year-on-year may be threatened. In addition, the application development and maintenance services on which the Indian IT industry has hitherto thrived are also increasingly facing commoditisation, leading to a squeezing of operating margins. This further emphasises the need to quickly find new vectors of differentiation and move up the value chain.

The pressure on operating margins applies to the North American and European software industries as well, but currently they are somewhat advantageously positioned because of their ability to do large, integrated, total outsourcing deals, which allow them to maintain an overall profitable margin. The Chinese software industry, however, already has a low operating margin currently because of its structure. This low operating margin in Chinese companies is due to the sub-optimal scale that is a result of a highly fragmented industry, with several thousand small players having on an average less than 100 employees.

The prominence of offshoring has given rise to the emergence of other low-cost nations, who are now competing with India to grab a slice of the global offshoring pie. So, while this is unlikely to pose any major threat to the Indian software firms in the next 3–5 years, India will surely see some of its share of offshoring going to the emerging destinations such as China, Eastern Europe, Mexico, The Philippines, Brazil, Russia and South Africa. Moreover, the MNCs – both the technology and product companies and the consulting and services companies – are rapidly expanding their bases in India, competing with Indian software firms on their own ground and playing by their rules to pursue global opportunities. As a result, large IT consulting and services firms such as IBM, Accenture, CSC, EDS, and Cap Gemini are able to position their offerings in as cost-competitive a manner as some of the leading Indian firms, and are able to influence large deals by leveraging their legacy brand and boardroom relationships. This cost-based positioning is likely to impact the operating margins of Indian companies unless they are quick to discover new sources of differentiation and offer compelling propositions to their clients through value migration. This is also likely to impact the flow of outsourcing business into China.

The growing MNC presence in India has also led to an intense war for talent, raising warning signs for a potential talent shortage that the Indian software industry might face. In addition, the Indian software industry is apprehensive that it may not get a sufficiently large and/or suitable talent pool to support its growth needs. Moreover, for high-end work such as

R&D and bioinformatics, people with higher qualifications such as PhDs are required, but Indian universities produce less than 300 PhDs in science, technology and engineering every year, when compared to 1,200 in China and higher numbers again in North America and Europe.

Moreover, the phenomenon of unbundling of large, billion dollar deals, from which the Indian software industry is set to gain, could also become a threat for the industry's business and credentials if the Indian vendors don't deliver the anticipated value proposition, because clients will then roll back to traditional total outsourcing deals.

The Indian software industry, like software industries elsewhere, also faces a threat from rapidly emerging technological paradigms such as utility computing, web computing, open source software and 'software as service' that are redefining the ways in which software is produced and consumed. Moreover, the emerging trends in software product design such as auto-configurability and 'self-service' integration also have the potential to eliminate some part of software services opportunities, although it will be a while before this materialises.

The Indian software and IT service industry operates through a combination of onsite and offshore staff. The onsite mode of work, which requires people to be located at customer sites (usually a foreign country), constitutes a significant part of the industry's manpower, as nearly 45 per cent of the industry's work is conducted onsite.[19] This ability to locate people onsite depends on the availability of applicable visas and work permits, and as such any change in immigration regulation poses a threat to the industry. In addition, the growing public and labour union opposition to offshoring is also a hindrance for the Indian software industry. For the North American and European software industries, this does not quite apply either because they are in the products business or because their services are consumed in domestic markets. The Chinese software industry, however, does stand to be affected by changes in immigration regulations.

Conclusions

The emergence of other 'software nations' on the global software industry landscape has certainly meant growing competition to the software and IT services industry in India. However, as the above SWOT analysis suggests, the combination of strengths and opportunities that the Indian software industry has far outweighs any negative impact that may arise in the event of its weaknesses and threats becoming real. The Indian software industry operates amidst a strong institutional framework and a vibrant capital market. A vast, high-quality, English-speaking young talent pool, superior operational capability, and a strong reservoir of structural, social and relationship capital lend strength to India's software industry. While the Indian software industry is not yet connected to software product market opportunities, it certainly has a strong upper hand when compared to the Chinese software industry, which suffers from high fragmentation and a weak institutional framework as well as a lack of credibility. The first-mover advantage the Indian software industry has will allow it to continue to stay ahead of the pack, especially in the realm of software and IT services. After almost two decades of development, China's software industry has shown its strength in high market growth and the government's strong support. How to overcome the weaknesses in managerial and technical skills and gain a significant market share in the ever-enlarging world software market remains a daunting task.

The next chapter explores some of the issues discussed in this chapter and relates them to segmentation within the global software industry. The fundamental dynamics of the software industry are discussed in relation to software research and development and the provision of products and services.

Further reading

Banerjee, P. (2004) *The Indian Software Industry: Business Strategy and Dynamic Co-ordination.* London: Palgrave Macmillan.

Heeks, R. (1996) *India's Software Industry.* New Delhi: Sage Publications.

Moitra, D. (2001) 'India's Software Industry', *IEEE Software*, January/February.

Notes

1. Saxenian, A.L. (2003) 'Government and Guanxi: the Chinese software industry in transition', CNEM working paper: 1.
2. 'Something New: Getting Serious About Innovation', *Economist*, August 3, 2006.

3. 'ExportIT China', US Department of Commerce Report, April 2003; available at *http://www.ita.doc.gov/media/Publications/pdf/exportit_china_2003.pdf* (accessed 21 November 2006).

4. Tschang, T. and Xue, L. (2003) 'The Chinese software industry: a strategy of creating products for the domestic market', ADB Institute working paper: 3.

5. Saxenian, op. cit.: 43.

6. Ibid: 43.

7. Tschang and Xue, op. cit.: 1.

8. Wall Street Journal (2006) 'Intel capital funds four Chinese firms', *Wall Street Journal Asian Edition*, June 27: c4.

9. This section is mainly based on 'ExportIT China', op. cit. Although this report is targeted at US small- and medium-sized IT firms, the information is useful for all the interested parties regardless of their country of origin.

10. Ju, D. (2001) 'China's Budding Software Industry' *IEEE Software* May/June.

11. Data available from various sources indicates that the average age of the talent pool in India is 24 years, when compared to 32 years in China. See, for example, *Outlook Business Magazine*, June 5, 2006.

12. Source: salary data, Mercer Human Resource Consulting, and others, including *http://news.bbc.co.uk/2/low/business/4436692.stm* (accessed 12 November 2006), *http://www.mercerhr.com/china-indiareport* (accessed 12 November 2006) and *http://www.todaysengineer.org/2004/Apr/outlook.asp* (accessed 14 November 2006).

13. Based on data gathered from patent offices and company annual reports.

14. The Indian software industry's annual revenue earning from the US is approximately 65 per cent.

15. Source: *Business Today*, March 26, 2006: 56–66.

16. Source: various reports.

17. Source: NASSCOM.

18. Source: various newspapers (*The Economic Times, The Hindu, The Times of India, The Tribune, Business Standard,* and *Deccan Herald*).

19. Source: *Dataquest*, 15 July 2006, Vol. XXIV(13).

5

Segmentation within the global software industry

Introduction

Within the software industry, globalisation refers to the extent to which firms target customers in markets within the industry throughout the world. Even within the same industry, globalisation of market presence can range from high to low depending on the firm's strategy and economic resources. According to Porter,[1] industry segmentation is the division of an industry into sections for the purposes of developing competitive strategy. Industry segmentation combines customer purchasing behaviour (market segmentation) with the behaviour of costs, both production costs and the costs of serving different customers. Segmentation encompasses the entire value chain. It exposes the differences in structural attractiveness among segments, and the conflicts in serving many segments simultaneously. In essence, segmentation is a division of an industry into subsidiary units whereupon such units can be analysed for the purpose of developing competitive strategies – a point we will return to in Chapter 7.

The benefits of segmentation undoubtedly vary from industry to industry and are to some degree dependent on the strategy that is adopted: for example, market niche, low cost or whether the product or service is in growth, maturity or decline. Although by no means exhaustive, market segmentation supports the development of competitive advantage in the following ways:

- It provides a realistic basis for targeting consumer and corporate markets.
- It focuses development of products and services that meet return on investment (ROI) within the market segments. Such market segments should provide greater ROI than those of competitors.

- It focuses the provider on achieving high levels of customer service and satisfaction.

- It assists decision makers to identifying gaps in the market.

- It encourages competitor analysis and helps identify strengths, weaknesses, opportunities and threats.

- It enables decision makers to gather market intelligence in a cost-effective manner.

- It provides a means and mechanism for decision makers to act quickly in highly competitive environments.

Although the software industry is a broad church of products and services, market segmentation only works if a product market already exists. As in the pharmaceutical industry, in the case of new technology one can only speculate as to who the early adopters might be. The ability to customise (and adapt) product and service offerings is quickly becoming a key differentiator in the software industry, and an advantage that China and India are acquiring over many Western firms.

Market segmentation

The fundamental dynamics of the software industry is characterised by firms engaged in software research and development and the provision of products and services. Classical theory on market segmentation was initially explained as a marketing strategy that firms choose to adopt. The concept of market segmentation was defined as viewing a heterogeneous market (one characterised by divergent demand) as a number of smaller homogeneous markets in response to differing product preferences among important market segments.[2] The goal of market segmentation is to describe such within-product category conditions that point to valued attributes and benefits.

Market segmentation has been the software industry's practical approach to finding the mechanism for the task of meeting consumer wants and needs. Consider, what is at issue? Regarding any one offering, management has resources to invest in responding to a finite set of consumer wants. Within a product category, it considers the diverse nature of wants, current state of want satisfaction – reflecting its own and competitive responses – and its likely ability to obtain a satisfactory return from supporting or continuing to support an offering. Providing information about consumer wants within a market is the task of market segmentation analysis (see Figure 5.1).

Figure 5.1   **Determinants of market opportunity**

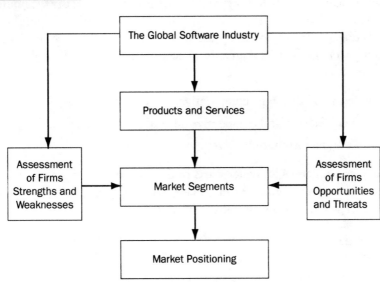

Source: adapted from Botten and McManus (1999).[3]

One of the benefits of using market segmentation is that it allows firms who operate at a global level to differentiate clusters of added value. As pointed out in Chapter 1, both China and India compete within a global industry and as such rely on close collaborations with partner organisations. Increasing competitiveness within market sectors requires individual firms to position their resources where they can best leverage added value and shareholder returns. For Chinese and Indian firms entering the software markets, or for existing firms, making decisions on how to position the firm and become competitive in a global market are important considerations.

As previously stated, segmentation is necessary to address the central question of competitive scope within an industry, or what segments of an industry a firm should serve and how it should serve them. It is also the basis for the choice of focus strategies, as it exposes segments that are poorly served by broadly-targeted competitors in which focus can be both sustainable and profitable. Broadly-targeted competitors must also understand industry segmentation, because it reveals areas where they are vulnerable to focusers and may suggest unattractive segments that are best left to competitors. Attention to segmentation from a strategic perspective is increasingly important, because new developments in technology are altering some of the old rules of segmentation, with implications for both focusers and broadly-targeted firms.

Chinese and Indian firms must think about the full range of environments in which they will compete and the entire economic spectrum of a business activity, including operations, suppliers, marketing, distribution and customer service. Only then can they identify strategic market segments, or economic activities, through which the firm can:

- establish an advantage comparative to the competition;
- define its market and competitive advantage over time; and
- secure stable profitability levels.

The question here is 'in which parts of the industry can firms expect the highest long-term returns?' In practical terms, within which market segments will it be possible for the firm to:

1. Develop a supportable advantage relative to competitors in other, possibly neighbouring segments?
2. Dispute competitors attractive returns on any investments required to enter the chosen segments?

The most important attribute of a strategic market segment is its defensibility. Evidence that a segment exists is the barriers to competition that surround it. So, for example, the higher the barriers, the higher the profit potential in that segment. Such barriers can (and will) include:

- trade barriers and taxation;
- capital investment;
- technology (patents and proprietary technology);
- location and infrastructure (for example, closeness to natural resources and transport facilities); and
- existing goodwill.

The nature of market segmentation involves firms designing products and services that satisfy smaller homogeneous groups of the total market (see Figure 5.2). Once these groups have been identified, and their needs understood, the firm may be able to develop a market mix appropriate for servicing a subgroup it considers a potential and profitable market. It could be argued however, that as we head towards the year 2010 firms should stop thinking of customers as part of an homogeneous market, and should instead consider customers as distinct, each of which requiring their own unique strategies in product policy, in promotional

| Figure 5.2 | Generic methods of market segmentation[7] |

Segmentation methods*	Physical attributes
Demographic	Sex, age, income, occupation, social class
Geographic	Countries, counties, cities, towns, rural areas
Buyer behaviour	When purchases are made, reasons for purchasing, purchasing influences, how purchasing is done
Psychographic	Belongers, achievers, emulators, I-am-me group, experiential, societal conscious, survivors, sustainers, and integrated*
Qualitative dimensions of the market	

Identification of best prospects by focusing on best segments:
    – Heavy users
    – Frequent purchasers
    – Firm intentions to buy soon
    – Good brand loyalty
    – Favourable attitudes towards brand
    – Segmentation, pin-pointing best
    – Prospects (from above)	

Conditions of market segmentation	

Differences between markets:
    – The degree of competition
    – The availability of substitutes
    – Consumer attitudes to the product
Degree of market power
    – Few providers (or sellers)
    – Product differentiation
Barriers to entry
    – Trade barriers
    – Standards and legislation
    – Control over distribution	

* To a large extent the plethora of factors used to define market segments reflects the difficulty of putting the normative theory of marketing segmentation into practice. The normative theory as proposed by Smith[8] is proactive in that one should use knowledge of customer characteristics to develop a marketing strategy. Whereas most marketing managers who use segmentation studies do so reactively in that they seek to determine the response of different marketing segments to their marketing strategies...a purist would argue that the managerial approach is more akin to product differentiation than a normative approach to marketing segmentation. See also Baker, M. (2000) *Marketing Strategy and Management*, 3rd Edition. Macmillan Business Press.
** These terms were developed by SRI International (formerly the Stanford Research Institute).

strategy, in pricing, in distribution methods and direct selling techniques (i.e. the 'everybody markets' – the philosophy of maximising the value of contact with each customer).

Evidence would suggest that future market strategies for China and India will need to be directed towards constantly-changing market needs. Under such conditions, market awareness, organisational flexibility, strategic vision, and external relationships are important strategic capabilities. Getting closer to the customer requires assessment of the customers needs and wants. The purpose of this assessment is to find an actual or potential competitive advantage.

Success in software markets

Both China and India have experienced varying degrees of success in their respective domestic and export markets. From Tables 1.3 and 1.4 in Chapter 1, our analysis of the Chinese and Indian software industries builds upon – and has been structured on the basis of – earlier models of national and software industry critical success factors. A generic model is that of Porter's[4] who sees key factors for industrial competitiveness as: demand conditions; local factor conditions; structure and strategy of local firms; and related/supporting industries.

Alongside this, we can set developing country-specific software models, which see key success factors as:

- human capital and costs, overseas linkages and diasporas, government policy;
- access to inputs, overseas linkages, firm clusters, firm-level strategy, government policy; national vision;
- government policy, geographic distribution of firms;
- skilled people, access to technology, structure and management of software firms, communication of information and knowledge;
- linkages and trust/transfers, industry clusters, access to inputs.

There is clearly overlap between these factors. For the purposes of initial analysis, these literature-derived critical success factors are synthesised into five factor dimensions: demand; national vision and strategy; international linkages and trust; software industry characteristics; and domestic input factors/infrastructure. For example, more than any other factor, software relies on people. Probably India's number one critical success factor has been the skills, expertise and size of the local labour pool. In part, this may be pre-existing – India has had strong scientific and technical establishments (including defence) since the 1950s. In part though, labour has been developed through deliberate government intervention to build the IT skills base, especially at the tertiary level, where all three have had and have strengthened excellent technical education institutions.[5]

At first sight, labour costs might seem to be central to software export success for India. While they have clearly been important, they need to be set alongside, rather than above, other factors. Survey evidence shows clients rate skills and the ability to close their labour demand–supply gap as more important than costs.

Two other human elements figure in India's success. The first is English, the global IT language, and also – not coincidentally – the language that dominates higher education and, to a significant degree, business. The second is knowledge. Initially through the diaspora but later through exports and client linkages, staff in Indian software exporters have built up a strong knowledge base: about overseas software markets, about overseas business norms and practices, and about specific customer needs and values. This has put them in a strong position to sustain and grow their software export business, whether in services or products.[6] In the next section, we will explore some of the issues identified and how these issues may affect China and India's market positions in the future.

China: defining the markets

Firms entering the software industry often begin by competing on a competitive wage structuring (cost differentiation). This allows firms to sell services that focus on the low-end of the value chain: this may include such activities as software coding. As firms develop domain expertise they move up the value chain and attract investment funds that allow them to develop market niches and attract FDI funding. Moving into niches is as much a first-mover as a late-entrant market strategy, and can bring with it many of the benefits of being first.

Chinese technology policy through the early 1990s favoured the large SOEs and government research institutes, following the model of Japan and Korea. However, most Chinese ministers lacked understanding of both the technologies that they sought to develop and the needs of Chinese industry, and Chinese SOEs and research institutes were unable to abandon the practices and structures of the planned economy. China also faced a different international environment than Korea and Japan had a decade or so earlier, one characterised by an accelerating pace of innovation and intensifying global competition. As a result, the strategies of the 1980s and early 1990s produced very little success.

Two decades of change in China's science and technology system have been both disruptive and remarkable at the same time. The Chinese economy is stronger today than most would have predicted back in the 1980s, with impressive achievements in building a national telecommunications infrastructure and widespread adoption of IT, particularly wireless telephones and related telecommunications products (Table 5.1). The new technology regime has been extremely successful in the development of IT manufacturing capabilities, where relationships between domestic firms and foreign investors – particularly from Taiwan and Hong Kong – have contributed to rapid development of the domestic capacity for low-cost manufacture of computers, consumer electronics, and communications equipment. While initially these ventures were restricted to low technology, labour-intensive processes, over time their technical capabilities have increased. China is now manufacturing laptop computers and sophisticated electronic components for export. In 2002, China ranked as the third-largest IT manufacturing centre in the world following only the US and Japan.[8]

Although China has outperformed India in many standard economic indicators, Chinese markets are still rudimentary and competition is economically and politically risky for firms. Software remains the weakest link in China's information technology sector. In the software sector, the key issues for individual companies revolve around inter-related questions that firms must answer to determine how they intend to compete. These questions include:

1. Where should the firm focus its marketing efforts, in the domestic or international markets? Alternatively;

2. How should the company focus its development efforts, in software services or software products?

Table 5.1   Adoption of IT in China and India

	Personal computers (per 1,000 people) in year 2000	Internet users (thousands) in year 2000	Internet secure services in year 2001	ICT expenditure (% of GDP) in year 2000	Telephone maintenance (per 1,000 people) in year 2000	Mobile phones (per 1,000 people) in year 2000
China	15.9	22,500	184	5.4	112	66
India	4.5	5,000	122	3.8	32	4

Source: Saxenian (2003).[9]

Domestic markets

In contrast to India, China has a strong domestic market. In the past 2–3 years China's domestic markets have benefited from the economic reforms that have taken place, especially those reforms that have influenced standards in product development.

There are approximately 20 million small to medium enterprises in China. In 2004, there were approximately 10,000 registered software firms employing around 600,000 people providing products and services in packaged software, financial services, security systems, electronic publishing educational and health-related products.[10]

Domestic Chinese software firms are typically characterised by the entrepreneur class, focused on niche markets that lack economy of scale. There is some clustering of software firms. Zhongguancuan Science and Technology Park in Beijing represents China's Silicon Valley, and is home to Oracle, IBM and Microsoft subsidiaries as well as dozens of other software firms. Beijing is by far the largest software-producing district, with a balanced industry including packaged, industrial, and security software as well as software for export. Beijing's prominence is in part due to its being a centre for government and leading educational and research institutions.

As of 2005, only a handful of firms have more than 1,000 employees or sales revenues in excess of $90 million. Foreign corporations, including Oracle, IBM, and Microsoft dominate the software product market in China. According to CCID,[11] the packaged software industry in China in 2005 reached $1.3 billion in sales, which provided 37,000 jobs and generated £220 million in tax payments. The top five packaged software vendors (PSV) accounted for 20 per cent of the market, though in recent years the internal Chinese market has seen a large number of new PSV opportunities, for example, the market for enterprise resource management software has increased tenfold in the last five years.

Although dominated by its domestic market strategy the Chinese software industry is moving forward on many fronts – today software services, primarily system integration, account for more than half of China's total software output and, despite the slow growth rates in some specialist software markets due to extreme rates of piracy in the industry, China does have some ambitious plans for the future as demonstrated by the following vision:

Vision: keywords in China's IT industry development for 2005[12]

1. Zero-duty.
2. Standards.

3. Innovation capability.

4. Marketing channel.

5. Capital operation.

6. Resource consolidation.

In more detail, these are:

1. *Zero-duty.* This will bring forth challenges as well as opportunities for the IT industry. In 2005, the 251 tax items related to IT products will all adopt zero-duty and this means both challenges and opportunities for domestic IT industry.

2. *Standards.* Standards on core technologies have already become an important influencing factor for China's IT industry development. On one hand, technological standards are the lifeline that determines the prosperity of an IT enterprise and a key information industry development index for the nation. On the other hand, disputes on domestic IT industry-related standards are becoming more and more intense. The domestic IT industry is eagerly awaiting the launch of the standards. As the final decision maker, the Ministry of Information Industry has also started to give active responses. It is believed that in 2005, these standards will show results.

3. *Innovation capability.* Innovation capability is crucial for domestic IT industry development in 2005. Under the background of the WTO and with the fast development of high-tech industry, the IT industry innovation capability will become a key factor for domestic IT industry development in 2005.

4. *Marketing channel.* This is a non-ignorable factor for domestic IT industry development in 2005. In the increasingly high market competition environment, those who have powerful channels will be the ones who can dominate favourable footings in competition and beat their competitors.

5. *Capital operation.* This is a new factor to influence IT industry development in 2005. Capital operation is not simple financing nor to be listed as an enterprise but is the process of generating abundant profit by modes of investment, penetration, merger, stock holding, etc. with its own capital.

6. *Resource consolidation.* This will exert great effect on IT industry development in 2005. Entering 2005, to merely rely on a single enterprise's own resources in the information era could not effectively

facilitate its participation in market competition. Modern enterprise competition has transformed from that between single enterprises to competition between one enterprise's supply chain and another such chain, which makes enterprise resource consolidate even more important.

Despite its charter for the future in terms of its domestic markets, many experts remain pessimistic about the future of the industry because of limited success in software product markets. Only by enhancing their product innovation capability, strengthening enterprise core-technology R&D, exploring effective marketing channels, improving enterprise capital operation capability and resource consolidation capability under the globalisation background can domestic IT enterprises get success.

Table 5.2	Top 10 Chinese software companies

Company	2002 sales (in millions of US Dollars)
Founder	438
PuTan	186
Legend	175
DongFang	134
ChongRan	126
ChongTian	125
TsingHua DongFang	115
Yian Tai	107
CVIC	94
Top	93

Source: CSIA Report, archive material from *http://www.idc.com/* (2002).

Table 5.3	China's top five PSV

Vendor	2002 sales (in millions of US Dollars)
IBM	78
Microsoft	65
Oracle	58
Sybase	31
Informix	26

Source: IDC Report, archive material from *http://www.idc.com/* (2002).

International markets

The importance of a global software vision for China was outlined in the previous section. The importance of vision in international markets cannot be underestimated. The most successful software firms (and exporters) have implemented their visions and sustained lead market positions in software products and services. Markets are comprised of many consumers, but consumers alone do not make a market. Markets require not only purchasers and a willingness to buy; they also need purchasing power and the authority to buy. Products and services for international markets are established activities for many western firms. The changing landscape however, and the composition of international markets and the emergence of new entrants and new organisational forms, are creating new pressures for both China and India.

Some Chinese firms have managed to establish strong international brands largely through partnerships, for example, the US firm Computer Associates partnership with NEUSOFT Group Limited, a software company based in Shenyang, in northeast China. The partnership aims to develop new-generation industrial solutions to better serve Chinese customers. The deepening of technological or other forms of capability is one way in which stronger Chinese firms differentiate themselves from their weaker rivals. For example, UFSoft and Kingdee are only the only software firms ranked among the top ten PSVs in China. As previously stated, there are a considerable number of firms that compete on cost alone, and although cost advantage is attractive to some consumers it may be a weakness when operating in the global market place. The more enlightened Chinese firms have attempted to move up the technological value chain, so as not to compete with the many smaller firms who could not compete at higher levels, but again this has its drawbacks: with the shortage of skilled professional software engineers the majority of Chinese companies are struggling to make their presence felt in many international markets.

In terms of magnitude, the biggest prizes lay within the international markets – stating the obvious, individual firms (or Western firms thinking of joint ventures) should undertake careful analysis to determine if they have the capabilities and resources to operate within international markets (see Table 5.4). China's future international standing and market position will be tested by many challenges. Such challenges include:

- Improving knowledge of the West and Western businesses practises;
- Improving product technology and service support;

- Improving market positioning to include:
  - reinforcement of existing positions
  - incremental repositioning
  - transformational repositioning
  - competitor de-positioning (this is the process of eroding a competitors position (India) of dominance)[13]
- Improving software capability (this includes process, technology and management capability);
- Improving English language capability;
- Increasing the number of university trained skilled software professionals;
- Increasing the rate of economic and trade reforms;
- Reducing its dependency on price for competitive advantage;
- Reducing dependency on state-owned enterprises;
- Reducing dependency on domestic markets;
- Reducing software piracy levels (to protect intellectual property rights).[14]

Emulating India's export success will not be easy; although it is easier said than done, at a macro level the prerequisites to entering the larger international and global markets must lay in the ability of Chinese firms to produce reliable technological products that are supported by legitimate intellectual property rights, procurement and finance regimes. Despite the challenges outlined above China appears to be making progress, albeit slow progress.

| Table 5.4 | Key criteria for choosing PSV[15] |

Key criteria	Response (%)
Cost	65
Commitment to quality	51
Flexible contract terms	39
References/reputation	34
Scope of resources	28

Note: The average length of an outsource contract is three years. Once the decision is made to outsource a function, it is highly unlikely that the function will be brought back in-house. At the end of the contract, approximately 40 per cent of outsource engagements are re-bid.

India: defining the markets

A key aspect of market segmentation is deciding which segments to choose and what resources are needed to market the products and services. Perhaps the most striking contrast with the Chinese software industry is India's strategic success in earning export revenues and research and development income. Given the relative population sizes of each country, one might have expected that the gulf between the two countries would have narrowed in time. However, although the strategies have converged to some degree, the cultural differences have not.

As a result of the technological fixation on software engineering, and the emphasis on cultural content of software as opposed to pure function, India has used its knowledge of Western business culture and its vast English-speaking population to enhance its market presence in many areas of product engineering and software services provision. For example, in the effort to make the development of software more cost-effective, Indian firms proceeded to standardise software engineering tools and environments and to re-use code in different projects.[17] This strategy culminated in advances in software engineering that were transferred into high-value software products. India's offshore capability has allowed it to take advantage of Western technology and innovations in software research and development. For example, software houses such as Tata Consultancy Services, Wipro, Infosys and others have gained significant expertise from the US and have benefited significantly from the establishment of dedicated offshore software development centres.

Evidence would suggest that whilst many large Western firms are moving their coding operations overseas, many of the offshore Indian software houses are pursuing aggressive and targeted strategies to expand their product and service market capabilities. As stated in Chapter 1, Indian firms want to be more than low-cost vendors; they want to be leaders in innovation. This may seem somewhat ambitious, but the following example is telling: Infosys and Wipro, two of the most successful Indian software firms, aim to provide software development services to US firms by developing their own products. Ranjit Singh,[18] a key figure in Xerox's Internet software development, put forward an explanation of this happening when he said 'that the limits of the arbitrage model that exploits offshore are being reached'.

Domestic markets

As stated in Chapter 1, the Indian computer software services industry has grown rapidly in the last 25 years, achieving record revenues of $2 billion in domestic earnings in 2002. From its early origins in the mid 1980s as a contract service provider to the US and Europe, India has been very successful in establishing a major domestic computer software and export services industry. For many years, the Indian software industry was considered a fringe provider by many multinational firms. India, however, quickly became a mainstream player delivering good quality software and services. Its strength being derived in part from its core capabilities in:

1. Software engineering: strong in software process, continually climbing the value chain.

2. English speaking management: strong management in top firms (high achievers from American Business Schools).

3. Product marketing: strong product branding high level of product support and distribution channels.

Unlike China, India's software firms are more clustered around the big cities such as Bangalore, Hyderabad, Mumbai (formerly Bombay), Pune, Delhi (India's capital in the north), Chennai, and Calcutta. Bangalore is by far the most vibrant of all software cities in India and is often referred to as India's 'Silicon Valley'.[19] There are varying accounts of how many software firms are actually located in Bangalore because of differing definitions of what constitutes software development. Altogether, it is estimated that there are approximately 220 software firms in Bangalore, the majority of which are medium-sized, i.e. between 100 and 150 employees, and only approximately 10 per cent of which have over 500 employees. More than two-thirds of the companies in Bangalore are Indian. There are also a wide range of software activities in Bangalore, from basic 'body-shopping' activities to cutting edge research. Bangalore has rapidly emerged as a software centre, surpassing Mumbai, one of the first software centres in India. Firms in Bangalore were among the first in India to react to the PC revolution. There is, therefore, a feeling that on the whole, the level of activities undertaken by the more established firms and the multinationals in Bangalore are more sophisticated and high-tech than in other cities in India.

Clustering has brought about a number of benefits: rapid interchange of information and knowledge, locational economies and a raised marketplace profile. Other benefits include:

- increased productivity and innovation;
- increased leverage over government policy;
- improved access to skilled employees and suppliers;
- improved brand imaging;
- improved access to global distribution;
- access to experts;
- access to institutional finance; and
- one-stop markets for international customers.

Within these clusters, there are many small-to-medium sized enterprises satisfying internal software markets for packaged system products in finance, education, video games and film. The larger domestic firms are steadily diversifying their activities. Although there is still a great deal of on-site work being done, industry people say that this is an important component of the process of software development. As the main market for Indian software exports is in the United States and involves primarily service-oriented activities, it is convenient for software professionals to spend some time in the environment for which they are developing software. This allows them to familiarise themselves with the client and what is to be achieved by the software. Many of the projects that are undertaken, therefore, may involve a segment of the work in one of the cities and a segment offsite. For example, apart from undertaking contract work in the form of producing specific segments of larger projects, Indian firms are increasingly getting involved in completing fixed-price turnkey projects in the area of customisation of software solutions. This entails sending professionals to the client to study the specifications of the system or the project. The work is then carried out and tested in India, and finally installed on-site.

International markets

Shortcomings in the domestic market have forced many of the Indian software firms to seek growth by moving into international export markets, mostly concentrated in United States and Europe. In terms of products and services, there have been continuous exports of software products since the early 1990s. Such products include enterprise systems and database tools, however, these product-based exports even today represent a small proportion of India's export capability; in essence India is still led by exporting services as indicated by Table 5.5. Tata Consultancy Services is the most dominant software force in India today.

For India, the nature of demand has been critical. As already noted in Chapter 1, the global software market has achieved double-digit growth for the past two decades. There has also been a huge gap between demand for, and supply of software labour (see Table 5.6) – accordingly, this has created a strong pull into the market.

With a constant flow of new entrants into the global software industry, profits from the sale of traditional services – for the Indian software industry at least – are likely to fall in the future; revenue growth would depend only on growth in the number of software workers. In order to survive the increased level of competition in the world market,

Table 5.5   **Top ten Indian software and services firms by revenue**

Firm	Revenue in Billions of US Dollars (2006)
Tata Consultancy Services	2.63
Infosys Technologies	2.04
Wipro Technologies	1.70
Satyam Computer Services	1.02
IBM Global Services (India)	0.77
HCL Technologies	0.73
Cognizant Technology Solutions (India)	0.57
Patni Computer Systems	0.48
Hewlett Packard (Global Delivery Centre India)	0.33
i-flex	0.32

Source: archive material from *Dataquest* Magazine *(http://www.dqindia.com)*.

Table 5.6   **Demand for software professionals**

	2002	2003	2004	2005	2006
Global Demand	360,000	635,000	850,000	1,065,000	1,200,000
India Supply	522,000	582,000	645,000	710,000	900,000

Source: archive material from *Dataquest* Magazine *(http://www.dqindia.com)*.

Indian firms, therefore would have to develop new products that are at the high end of the value chain. In this context, while India's largest software service firms, Tata, Wipro and Infosys, reported significant increases in profits in the last few years they have experienced increasing competition from a number of low-cost Asian nations such as Vietnam. India also faces challenges within its labour markets – historically, there has been a high premium placed on talent without a sense of ownership that has led to a high attrition rate amongst software professionals; this in turn has led to restricted scope and chances for growth in high-value market sectors such as telecommunications or infrastructure services. Firms such as Wipro have established their own training hubs and learning centres to combat this threat. Strategies[20] include:

- continuous learning opportunities and increasing employability;
- high quality of work and work life;
- overseas assignments;
- competitive compensation and pay performance;
- wealth-creation opportunities;
- learning support; and
- career progression and management.

To stay competitive, many firms have established human-resource differentiators that go beyond the work environment and look at employees' personal, social, and family needs. Although calculations do differ, global demand for software professionals is estimated to reach record levels in 2006 (see Table 5.6). By 2006, the Indian labour pool will be approximately 900,000 professionals. As supply potentially falls short of demand, wage rates are likely to increase: this will inevitably put pressure on some of India's cost differentiated markets, and will certainly put pressure on firms such as Tata as US and European firms look for alternative sources for their offshoring activities.

Evidence would also suggest that many large Indian firms are developing expertise in the so-called vertical domain areas because they offer a hike up the value chain into areas of work that are longer-term and more lucrative than traditional code programming.[21] In addition, aggressive attempts have been made by a small number of Indian companies to globalise, through acquisition by setting up overseas development sites or by acquiring a 'front-end' marketing capability. One challenge of acquisition is managing the process of absorption. This is a useful cultural test for Indian companies, whose takeovers and mergers have typically been confined to targets owned by fellow Indians, albeit living in the US. Reasons for acquisitions beyond getting a toe-hold in the market include ready resources, clients and revenues. We should also add access to new sets of skills or domain and process expertise in the target market, access to a new technology or intellectual property and also greater credibility with target clients, by having a strong local presence beyond just a sales office.

Conclusions

It is easy to argue that Indian firms will continue to gain market share even if they have only a small share of the global market; however, it is different to suggest the same if India's market share is high (say 15 per cent or above). India may still gain market share because of cost arbitrage. It is, however, no longer as easy because the impact of the macro environment is much higher. Given this situation, the underlying market strategy seems to be to build in scale to meet a rise in outsourcing in the long term, primarily from global telecoms companies that have yet to fully embrace the Indian offshore model.

Notes

1. Porter, M. (1985) *Competitive Advantage*. Macmillan Free Press; p. 231.
2. Smith, W.R. (1956) 'Product differentiation and market segmentation as alternative marketing strategies', *Journal of Marketing*, 3(8): 6.
3. Botten, N. and McManus, J. (1999) *Competitive Strategies for Service Organisations*, Macmillan Business Press; p. 60.
4. Porter, M. (1990) 'The competitive advantage of nations', *Harvard Business Review*, March–April: 73–93.
5. The result, for example, is a higher numbers of scientists, engineers and technicians per head of population than in neighbouring countries (UNDP, 2001).
6. Source: Heeks, R. (2002) 'Software export success factors and strategies in developing and transitional economies', *IDPM*, paper 12.
7. Source: Botten and McManus, op. cit.: 61.
8. Smith, op. cit.
9. Saxenian, A.L. (2003) *Global Software from Emerging Markets: an Engine for Growth*. London Business School.
10. The World Bank, 2002 World Development Indicators.
11. Source: China Software Industry Association.

12. CCID Market research centre affiliated with the Ministry of Electronics Industry.
13. Source: Industry News China Software Industry Association, September 20, 2005.
14. A full account of positioning may be found in the work of Hooley, G. (2000) 'Positioning', in *Market Theory,* ed. M. Baker. London: Thomson Learning; pp 181–205.
15. To boost enforcement in the face of growing international pressure, on December 23, 2004, China's highest courts announced a stricter interpretation of China's existing IPR laws. According to the courts, China has lowered the threshold for punishable offences to USD 6,000 from USD 12,000–24,000, and has increased prison sentences from three to seven years. And for the first time, dissemination of pirated goods or software over the Internet is explicitly forbidden.
16. Outsourcing Institute Fifth Annual Report, 2005. The average gross annual revenues of the participants/respondents' companies is $1 billion, but the median is closer to $231 million.
17. With the exception of the United States, India has the largest concentration of level 5 CMMI-accredited firms.
18. Comments made at the workshop on global software development, Reginald H. Jones Centre, Wharton School, December 1999.
19. Sharma, A. (1994) 'Bangalore: the Silicon Valley of India', *Software Today,* October: 84–8.
20. Deependra, M. (2001) 'Country report: India's software industry', *IEEE Software,* 78.
21. Merchant, K. (2001) 'IT Sector hopes it can turn problems into solutions', *FTIT,* February.

6

Interrelationships in China and India's software industries

Introduction

This chapter covers two topics: the first at the company level – the business scope and geographic reach of a software firm; the second at the industry level – the phenomenon of clustering of software and related firms in one particular location. These two topics are grouped together as both are closely related with interrelationships.

Firms make their decisions on the scope of businesses and on the breadth of geographic reach based on 'synergy'. The first topic will be analysed using Porter's framework of interrelationships and horizontal strategies and Khanna's theory of institutional void in emerging economies. As for the second topic, built on Porter's theory of cluster, a comparison of India's Banglore IT cluster and China's software parks will try to address the following questions:

1. What roles have the software parks played in the development of China and India's software industries?
2. Putting the software parks in a broader perspective, what does it take to foster an IT cluster?
3. What should be the appropriate roles of the government and institutions in the development of the software industry, especially in the case of emerging economies like China and India?

While Porter's original idea on competitor interrelationships was about how a diversified company matches its competitor's choices of product portfolio in order to gain and maintain competitive advantage, we view interrelationships in a broader sense that refers to interaction and collaboration between firms. In particular, the following three types of interrelationships are identified as being important for the development of China and India's software industries:

- the ones between domestic software firms;
- the ones between software firms and other related IT firms; and
- the ones between multinational corporations and domestic software firms.

Above all, the government and other institutions for collaboration also play important roles in the development of China and India's software industries.[1]

Interrelationships and horizontal strategies of software firms

Porter applies the ideas of interrelationships and horizontal strategies to the analysis of corporate strategy. The major issue is how to leverage the synergy across different value chains in the hope of making the total value of the diversified company higher than the summation of individual business's values as they stand alone. According to Porter, interrelationships are not the fuzzy notions of fit but tangible opportunities to reduce costs or enhance differentiation in virtually any activity in the value chain. There are three types of interrelationships: tangible relationships, intangible relationships and competitor interrelationships. While tangible interrelationships arise from opportunities to share activities in the value chain, intangible interrelationships involve the transference of management know-how among separate value chains and competitor interrelationships stem from the existence of rivals who actually or potentially compete with the company in more than one business unit.

In terms of corporate strategy, one critical issue is how to define the strategic business units (SBU). Cusumano categorises the business of software into three types: product, service and mix.[2] Therefore, the unit of analysis can be started from a business unit producing one particular software product or providing one particular type of software service. Evidence shows that more and more software firms are mixed in the sense that they provide both products and services. In the software industry, interrelationships exist between products, between services and between products and services.

Porter also uses similar reasoning exploring the issues of globalisation and firms' competition across borders. Firms considering internationalisation must pay attention to the issue of how they can leverage their competitive advantage in their home countries and extend it into the global arena, i.e. take advantage of synergies across locations. As a first step, it is important to understand the differences between a multi-domestic and a global industry. In multi-domestic industries, competition in each country (or small groups of countries) is essentially independent of competition in other countries. The definition of a global industry is an industry in which a firm's competitive position in one country is significantly affected by its position in other countries and vice versa. The implications of competitive strategies are quite different for a multi-domestic and a global industry. In a multi-domestic industry, the firm's international strategy should be a 'country-centred strategy': international strategy collapses to a serious of domestic strategies. In a global industry, a company must in some way integrate its activities on a worldwide basis to capture the linkages among countries. The integration will require more than simply transferring intangible assets among countries, though it will include such transfer. All the important competitors in the global industries compete worldwide with increasingly coordinated strategies.[3]

One mistake often made by firms going international is that they apply 'global strategies' on multi-domestic industries. Rather than doing research on the unique business environment of a country or region and designing specific, tailored strategy, they try very hard to consolidate and integrate branding, marketing, distribution channels etc. The pioneer Chinese firms that expanded abroad such as Lenovo, TCL, Huawei all have learned this lesson the hard way.[4]

Considering the case of software, again the issue worth thinking about is whether software is a global industry, i.e. is a firm's competitive position in one country significantly affected by its position in other countries or vice versa. Given the characteristics of the software industry and the current positioning of Chinese and Indian software firms, will internationalisation need to apply global strategies or multi-regional strategies? For example, to what extent can Indian firms leverage their success in the outsourcing business in the US market and extend it to other countries and regions? Many Chinese software firms that have successfully won Japanese outsourcing contracts have the ambitious goal of extending their success into the US and European markets, to compete with the incumbent Indian firms in these markets. Whether these hopes can become reality depends to a large extent on the firms' correct understanding of this issue, and therefore adoption of the right mix of strategies.

Here, naturally, we need to consider the market segments of the software industry as described in Chapter 7. Some segments of the software industry, such as packaged software, are global, but other segments such as consulting services are multi-domestic. There is no doubt that Microsoft is selling its Windows operating systems and Office suite in the international market, and so it needs a truly global strategy. By contrast, even large consulting firms with global brands such as Accenture, PriceWaterhouseCoopers (PWC), KPMG have to localise their strategies and compete with local small firms in different countries. But it is worth mentioning that it is not an either/or issue when a company chooses an international strategy: in most cases it is somewhere between a pure international strategy and a pure multi-domestic strategy. In order to illustrate this point, we will consider the business strategies of the two major IT service companies competing worldwide, SAP and Oracle. Both firms generate their revenue through the selling of packaged software products and customised services. For the most part, SAP encourages users to adopt the procedures and data definitions built into its products, rather than adapt the software to user procedures and data.[5] As a comparison, Oracle seems to rely more on customisation of its products and services in order to adapt to the local needs.

Interrelationships ultimately stem from commonalities of various types among industries, such as common buyers, channels, or production processes. These commonalities define potential interrelationships. Whether the interrelationships lead to a competitive advantage is a function of the benefits and costs involved.[6]

The growing sophistication of information systems is a powerful force in opening up possibilities for interrelationships. With the increasing capacity to handle complex data online, information technology is allowing the development of automated order processing systems, automated materials handling systems, automated warehouses, and systems to automate other value activities outside of manufacturing. These systems can often be shared among related businesses. Information technology is also restructuring distribution channels, and the selling process in industries such as banking and insurance, in ways that facilitate sharing. At the same time that technology is creating interrelationships, it is also reducing the costs of exploiting them. The ease of communication has increased just as dramatically as its costs have fallen, reducing the costs of coordinating the activities of business units.[7] The success of the Indian software and services outsourcing industry would have been impossible without the high-quality infrastructure provided in the software development parks. The greatest challenge for Indian companies in the 1980s was the lack of international telecommunications links that are the necessary infrastructure for software exports. Without reliable telecommunications links, Indian firms had no alternative to providing contract programming on-site (at the customer's facilities), typically in the US. One of the contributions of the Software Development Parks (STP) was that it provided a basic infrastructure including core computer facilities, reliable power, ready-to-use office space, and communications facilities such as 64 Kbps data lines and Internet access.[8]

Tangible interrelationships

Tangible interrelationships arise from opportunities to share activities in the value chain among related business units. The advantage of introducing the notion of a value chain is to break up the activities of the company and then formulate the strategies of the company. Competitive advantage lies in the superior performance in difference segments of the value chain, either in the form of reduced costs or more focused differentiation. According to Porter, a business unit can potentially share any value activity in the value chain with another business unit in the company, including both primary and supporting activities. Certain raw materials can be procured and handled jointly, the development of technology on products and processes is shared, a joint sales force sells both products, and both products are shipped to buyers via the same physical distribution system, etc. Sharing a *large* value activity leads to a competitive advantage if it affects the drivers of cost position or differentiation.

Sharing will have a material impact on overall cost position only if the value activities involved are a significant proportion of operating costs or assets. Sharing affects differentiation in two ways. It can enhance differentiation by increasing the uniqueness of an activity, or it can lower the cost of differentiation.

Porter divides forms of sharing into five categories and therefore identifies five types of tangible interrelationships: market inter-relationships, production interrelationships, procurement relationships, technological interrelationships and infrastructure interrelationships. Although these generic interrelationships apply to all the industries, for the software industry – and especially for China and India's software industries – the most important ones are market interrelationships, technological interrelationships and infrastructure interrelationships. The first two help open up new market opportunities and the last one addresses the weaknesses in software industry development in developing countries.

In the software industry, buyers and technological changes are two major driving forces for the realisation of interrelationships. Buyers, themselves under pressures such as requiring one-stop shopping or unified solutions, are often a force for coordination; therefore market interrelationships arise as a result. Facing the same buyers, primary value activities involved in reaching and interacting with the buyer can be shared: shared brand name, shared advertising, shared promotion, shared marketing department, shared channel, shared sales force, shared service network etc.

Technological change is proliferating interrelationships and making them more achievable. Technology is breaking down barriers between industries and driving them together, particularly those based on electronics/information technology. Microelectronics, low-cost computers and communications technology are permeating many businesses and causing technologies to converge. As these technologies are assimilated into many products and production processes, the opportunities for shared technology development, procurement, and component fabrication are increasing.[9]

Infrastructure interrelationships include sharing in such activities and areas as finance, legal, accounts, and human resource management. In China and India's software industries, identifying and leveraging infrastructure interrelationships is extremely important. Due to the inefficiency of capital markets in China and India, joint raising of capital and shared utilisation of capital are very important for software firms. Other forms of infrastructure interrelationships such as shared hiring and training, and shared government relations are also important. As we discuss later on, the building of software parks in China and India have been the results of efforts in building infrastructure interrelationships for the development of their software industries.

The software industry is highly knowledge based and labour intensive, and therefore intangible interrelationships and competitor interrelationships are equally if not more important than tangible interrelationships.

Intangible interrelationships

Intangible interrelationships lead to competitive advantage through the transfer of skills among separate value chains. Intangible interrelationships are important to competitive advantage when the transfer of know-how or skills allows the receiving business unit to lower costs or enhance differentiation.

The software industry has huge economies of scale and a significant learning curve, therefore the experience of success can bring good intangible interrelationships when a company enters a new line of business or enters a new location. Almost all the top Indian software companies have built subsidiaries in China hoping that their success in the software outsourcing business can be transferred to the marketplace in China by leveraging the huge pool of cheap software personnel available. However, as Porter put it, the most common pitfall in assessing intangible interrelationships is to identify generic similarities among business units that are not important to competition, and many firms have fallen into the trap of identifying intangible interrelationships that are illusionary or do not matter for competitive advantage.[10] Given the differences in China and India's macro and micro environments for the software industry, it will be interesting to see whether Indian software firms can achieve similar success in China as in India, no matter whether they intend to serve the Chinese markets or use China as an export base.

Competitor interrelationships

Porter's ideas on 'competitor relationships' refer to where 'firms actually or potentially compete in more than one industry'. In the cases of tangible and intangible interrelationships, this is how to leverage common resources but not include competitors. Multipoint competitors link industries together.

The evolution of the PC industry clearly demonstrates the transformation of competitor interrelationships among computer firms. The rise of the 386 marked a growing interdependence among firms in the computer industry. Former Intel CEO Andy Grove argued that in the 1980s, the computer industry was transformed from a vertical alignment based on the exclusive use of proprietary technologies, to a horizontal alignment with open standards. As he put it, 'a vertical computer company had to produce computer platform and operating systems and software. A horizontal computer company, however, supplies just one product. By virtue of the functional specialisation that prevails, horizontal industries tend to be more cost-effective than their vertical equivalents.'[11]

The proliferation of the Internet is further dramatically reshaping the competitor interrelationships among IT firms. Recent research by Accenture highlights the dramatic change in the enterprise software value chain caused by the Internet, which is termed the industrialisation of the value chain.[12] With the advent of the Internet, the full hierarchy of participants in business activities – every kind of company, department, employee, customer and consumer – could at last be on the same network, collaborating and transacting with each other. Across applications, system management and development tools, vendors invented new use cases (e.g. customer self-service) and re-invented old ones (e.g. order management) for the new networked world. The Internet has begun rewriting the rules of the enterprise software game and the very definition and design of the software product by fostering two highly significant developments: firstly, a steady increase in the adoption of a growing set of open standards for Internet-based computing by all vendors, and secondly, acceleration of a re-architecture of software using Service Oriented Architecture (SOA). Armed with open standards, SOA, and the Internet as their distribution mechanism, a global cottage industry of small software developers will package and distribute useful intellectual property as application services (many of which will complement offerings from the large vendors). The Internet is building a global bridge to the seemingly unlimited masses of development talent around the world, inviting them to enter the market. In an industrialised value chain, SOA is a critical element – the 'production blueprint' – due to its built-in interoperability of software components. With interoperability, tasks such as design, development and testing can be decoupled and distributed, and can be assigned most efficiently to local and offshore labour. Clearly these technological revolutions will redefine interrelationships in the software industry and bring otherwise non-existing opportunities to software players in China and India.

Horizontal strategy and competitive advantage

After identifying all the interrelationships between business lines and between locations, the company needs to formulate a horizontal strategy about diversifying its businesses or about entering new geographical locations. Horizontal strategy is a set of coherent long-term objectives and action programs aimed at identifying and exploiting interrelationships across distinct but related business units. It is the mechanism by which a diversified company enhances the competitive advantage of its business units. There are a number of organisational barriers to achieving interrelationships in practice, which are difficult to surmount even if the strategic benefits are clear. Without organisational mechanisms to facilitate interrelationships that work in tandem with a decentralised corporate organisational structure, horizontal strategy will fail.

In Chapter 3 on China and India's SWOT analysis, we argue that one of the weaknesses of the Chinese software industry is the software firms' small sizes that make them unable to realise economies of scale. Some of China's industry insiders are now proposing the idea of software alliances in order to overcome this weakness. To what extent this effort will be successful still remains to be seen; if interrelationships among value chains in the same firm are difficult to surmount, clearly there will be more difficulties in harnessing interrelationships across firms that are cooperating purely based on the prospect of mutual benefit.

One common feature of China and India's software industries is that the dominant firms in the software and service industries are conglomerates that have built their presence in a variety of businesses and have broad geographic reach. For example, China's leading computer hardware manufacturers such as Legend and Great Wall are active in the IT services market because they see it as a way of expanding beyond their original businesses. In fact, there are very few specialised and dedicated Chinese software providers. Many of the largest software developers in China are diversified IT firms, such as Founder and Legend. Telecommunications equipment manufacturers, for example Huawei and Zhongxing, are among the largest software producers in China because they develop most of their own software internally.[13] Spanning most sectors of the Indian economy, the Tata companies employ close to 300,000 people and had sales of US$8.6 billion in the fiscal year 1995 to 1996. Of the group's 90 companies, more than 40 are publicly traded, and they account for approximately 8 per cent of the total capitalisation of the country's publicly-traded companies. The companies are all held together by the internationally-recognised Tata name and by interlocking investments and directorates.[14]

These observations seem at odds with the focused strategies prescribed in a typical strategy textbook. Khanna and Palepu's research findings can give us some clues to understand these phenomena: it is the institutional void that may make the focused strategies not work in such emerging economies as China and India. Companies must adapt their strategies to fit their institutional context – a country's product, capital, and labour markets, its regulatory system, and its mechanisms for enforcing contracts. Emerging economies fall short to varying degrees in providing the institutions necessary to support business operations. In emerging economies, highly diversified business groups can be particularly well suited to the institutional context: conglomerates can add value by imitating the functions of several institutions that are present only in advanced economies. Successful groups effectively mediate between their member companies and the rest of the economy. In the product markets, as a result of lack of information, companies in emerging markets face much higher costs in building credible brands than their counterparts in advanced economies. In turn, established brands wield tremendous power. A conglomerate with a reputation for quality products and services can use its group name to enter new businesses. In the capital markets, almost all the institutional mechanisms that make advanced capital markets work so well are either absent or ineffective in emerging markets. Having little information and few safeguards, investors are reluctant to put money into new enterprises. In such a context, diversified groups can point to their track record of returns to investors. As a result, large and well-established companies have superior access to capital markets. They can also use their internally-generated capital to grow existing businesses or enter new ones. Similar advantages favouring conglomerates also exist in the labour markets and in the government relationships.

One interesting phenomenon in the world IT industry is that firms tend to congregate in a particular location, such as the Silicon Valley in the US and Bangalore in India. In China, intentional efforts from both government and from business are aiming to create geographical IT clusters such as the ones mentioned above.

According to Porter's definition, a cluster is a geographically proximate group of interconnected companies and associated institutions in a particular field, linked by commonalities and complementarities. The geographical scope of a cluster can range from a single city or state to a country or even a network of neighbouring countries.[15] Clusters affect competition in three broad ways: first, by increasing the productivity of constituent firms or industries; second, by increasing their capacity for innovation and thus for productivity growth; and third, by stimulating new business formation that supports innovation and expands the cluster. Porter models the effect of location on competition using four interrelated influences, graphically depicted in a diamond, a metaphor that has become a shorthand reference to the quality of a location's business environment: factor (input) conditions, demand conditions, related and supporting industries, and context for company strategy and rivalry.

The phenomenon of IT clusters and software parks in China and India can also be seen as efforts by the government and the businesses to leverage interrelationships and overcome the institutional void in the effort of building IT clusters. In the next section, we will describe the evolution and current situations of China and India's software clusters: India's Bangalore and China's software parks.

Software clusters in China and India

Saxenian compares the situations of Bangalore and the Silicon Valley and concludes that India will need a broader vision for its IT industry, and to define its own pathway in the IT era. Silicon Valley emerged in the post-war US economy with the advantage of a large domestic market, a widely-educated population, and well-functioning infrastructure and regulatory institutions. The same factors have facilitated the swift diffusion of information technology into the US economy and society – and supported a virtuous cycle of technological innovation to meet the needs of local producers and consumers. In comparison, the task for Indian policymakers who aspire for IT to become more than an enclave in an otherwise backward economy is to develop a wider range of industries and institutions to support the economic and spatial diffusion of IT.[16]

For both China and India, the future of their software industries lies in the prospective of becoming an integrated part of the global IT industry, and becoming an engine to drive the whole economy. Currently the two countries' IT clusters are far behind the Silicon Valley example, but in the long run it may be more likely we will see some genuine IT clusters emerging in China earlier than in India, based on a comparison of the two countries' 'diamond' conditions: China has stronger and more sophisticated domestic demand and better related and supporting industries. If we can say that China and India score even in factor conditions, maybe India is stronger in the context for company strategy and rivalry.

Bangalore: an Indian IT cluster[17]

Originally a software export base, after several decades of development, Bangalore is now on its way to becoming a fully-fledged high-technology cluster. It is now playing host to firms manufacturing machine tools, telecoms equipment, electronic products and auto components. In recent years, Bangalore has also emerged as a premier bio-tech cluster in the country. Often claimed to be the Silicon Valley of India, the success story of Bangalore has attracted a great deal of academic research; here we want to emphasise one aspect of the story, namely the interrelationships in Bangalore: the ones between firms and other institutions and the ones between multinational corporations and domestic firms.

Role of the government and organisations in Bangalore

In contrast with China's government-driven approach to IT development, the Indian government has been less interventional: 'until 1991–1992, there was virtually no policy support at all for the software sector. Even the term "benign neglect" would be too positive a phrase to use in this connection.'[18] But the government did facilitate the industry by creating infrastructure support. The Software Technology Parks (STP) scheme introduced by the Department of Electronics (DoE) in the early 1990s insured that the infrastructure and administrative support for exporting were available in India, and therefore the STP scheme facilitated a gradual shift away from on-site to offshore service provision in the 1990s.

The roles played by NASSCOM have been critical for the development of the Bangalore cluster: it has successfully brought together businesses and the government, addressed the common needs of all the businesses such as infrastructure, overseas connections etc. The active role of NASSCOM in shaping policy distinguishes the software industry from the computer hardware and other older Indian industries. NASSCOM has been influential in shaping the DoE strategy of working with software companies to provide critical infrastructure, while explicitly avoiding more detailed regulation or intervention. For example, the DoE's decision to organise the STPI program as an autonomous unit and eventually to privatise it has been influenced by the lobbying of NASSCOM.[19]

Interrelationships between multinational corporations and domestic firms in the cluster

Multinational corporations started to enter the Bangalore cluster in the 1980s. Texas Instruments (TI) was a pioneer in this endeavour, and showed the potential of offshore activities in a significant manner.

Because TI persisted with their vision of having a unit in India and managed to deal with all the bureaucratic hassles such as ensuring Internet connectivity, etc., it inspired other firms to do the same. The rate of entry of MNCs accelerated after the late 1980s. Out of the 77 multinational corporations that have established their R&D centres as direct subsidiaries in India, 40 are located in Bangalore, making it far ahead of other locations.[20]

These MNCs contribute to the local cluster through training and collaborations with local firms and educational institutions. Almost all the MNCs in Bangalore have set up their own training centres. The linkage of these MNCs with local firms has facilitated the learning process and has enhanced the capabilities of the Bangalore cluster. One major source of capability creation in the cluster has been linkages between small IT firms and the MNCs.

Evidence shows that the Indian firms such as Wipro and Infosys have forged alliance with MNCs to conduct advanced activities. Small firms also collaborate with MNCs through offering workforce for the MNCs and larger Indian firms on a project-by-project basis.

Software park development in China[21]

Origins of China's software parks: government initiated projects

Aiming at fostering the necessary environment for the development of China's software industry, in the 1980s the Chinese government started to initiate the creation of national high-tech industrial development zones that provide firms with first rate infrastructure (such as roads, buildings, telecommunications and high speed Internet connections, electrical facilities etc.) and a variety of preferential taxes and collective services. In 1995, the Ministry of Science and Technology (MOST) selected some software parks and software firms as the target of favourable support, which was termed the 'Torch program'. By the end of 2000, the Torch program has designated 19 software development bases, covering more than 1,000 software firms, 90,000 software personnel and more 80 per cent of the total revenue in that year.[22]

In 2001, the Ministry of Information Industry announced a plan to re-centralise resources in the software industry in hopes of enhancing competitiveness. They have identified 11 National Software Industrial Bases located in Beijing, Shanghai, Dalian, Chengdu, Xi'an, Jinan, Hangzhou, Guangzhou, Changsha, Nanjing and Zhuhai. These 11 areas are entitled to receive preferential policies including venture capital, funding, support services, and assistance in being listed on the stock exchange. This represents part of an effort to reinforce the existing concentration of IT-related industries in the urban centres in the Eastern and Middle regions of China, and should reinforce the already existing agglomeration of the software industry among the coast. By 2002, China had a total of 48 software development parks dispersed widely around the country.

In 2003, the National Development and Reform Committee, the Ministry of Information Industry, and the Ministry of Commerce jointly designated six national-level software export bases including Zhongguancun Software Park, Tianjin Huayuan software export base, Dalian Software Park, Shanghai Pudong software Park, Xian Software Park and Shenzhen Software Park.

Two case studies of software parks: Zhongguancun and Dalian

Among the eleven national software industrial bases, the Zhongguancun Software Park is towards the upper end of the value chain. Zhongguancun Software Park Development Co, Ltd. (zPark) was founded in August 2000, with sponsorship and underwriting by Beijing's municipal government. zPark was established as a planning, construction, and property-management committee with the sole mission of overseeing zPark's development and operation. zPark is located in China's version of Silicon Valley – Zhongguancun. zPark is devoted to being a service platform to help its customers to succeed. In addition to providing the best working environment possible, zPark invested heavily in offering value-added business services for its tenants. zPark is also focused on high-tech R&D and facility hosting, as well as providing consulting and IT services on a global basis; furthermore, since 2001 it has been certified as one of China's 11 national-level software parks. Every year, there are over 200 international or domestic business groups visiting zPark. In establishing itself as the clear leader and centre of China's software industry, zPark has developed a comprehensive, professionally managed high-tech support platform hosting operations for both domestic and international software vendors and system integrators. As collateral missions, zPark is devoted to assisting China's general efforts of internationalisation, as well as propelling China's software industry into world markets.

As a pioneer in China's technology parks, zPark has attracted many heavyweight domestic and international companies. More than 120 domestic and multinational software companies have already established operations in zPark. In this mix, there are 22 R&D centres from such renowned international and domestic enterprises as Oracle, Siemens, Iona, Harbor Networks, etc. In addition, 98 small- and medium-sized companies have established businesses in the Park's incubation centre, which is steadily growing in both headcount and revenue.

zPark-customer companies presently employ 8,700 professionals, contributing revenue of 8 billion RMB in 2003. Upon its completion at the beginning of 2006, zPark estimates an employee base of 30,000 people, generating annual revenues of 13.2 billion RMB. Current customer companies offer a wide range of software products and IT services covering the following industries:

- financial/accounting;
- telecommunications;
- e-business;
- education;
- public services;
- manufacturing, both process and discreet;
- distribution;
- healthcare.

The Dalian software park has a clear software export orientation, and has the ambition of becoming *the* offshoring centre of service outsourcing in northeast Asia. Located in the Higher Education and Culture Zone of Dalian, the Dalian Software Park is surrounded by numerous universities and research institutes. After its establishment in 1998, the Dalian Software Park was certified and approved by the Ministry of Science and Technology as a key base for the 'State High-Tech Torch Plan for Software Industry' and Dalian as the 'Model City for Internationalisation of the Software Industry'. As one of the 11 'National Software Industry Bases' and one of the five 'National Software Export Bases' in China, Dalian Software Park has the honour of being the national software park featuring the highest level of development and internationalisation.

Supported by preferential governmental policies, numerous pools of talented IT personnel, ample funding and an active market, Dalian Software Park provides an exceptional setting for both domestic and overseas software, BPO and ITES enterprises. Currently, around 200 enterprises have settled in Dalian Software Park, of which foreign enterprises account for over 41 per cent. Half of all enterprises in the park are engaged in software, BPO and ITES outsourcing services for North Asia and other regions. Thirty Global 500 corporations such as GE, IBM, HP, Dell, Matsushita, Sony, Toshiba, Accenture and SAP to name but a few, including some Japanese software or BPO-related companies such as Omron, CSK, Alpine, Furuno Softech, FTS and Sino-Japan Engineering have established R&D centres here, for either North Asia or global markets. Neusoft, CS&S, Sunyard and many other renowned domestic software enterprises have set up their export bases here for the North Asian markets of Japan and Korea.

Dalian Software Park is growing to be the 'The Offshoring Center of Service Outsourcing in Northeast Asia' by targeting the markets of Japan, Korea, the greater China area and ASEAN, a global resources centre of multinationals to serve and support their Northeast Asia operations and the American and European markets. Dalian Software Park works towards continued internationalisation through the attraction of both international and domestic software, BPO and ITES companies, as well as becoming the largest software export base and the largest professional software training base in China.

Achievements of the parks and problems faced

Despite the good intention of the government's promotion of the software industry, clearly we see some problems in these initiatives. The strong roles played by the different levels of government are a double-edged sword. On one hand, it does heighten awareness throughout the whole of society about the importance of software in a region's economic development. But on the other hand, overinvestment and a waste of resources has occurred from a national perspective. The high-profile promotion by central government puts pressure on local authorities that makes them feel they are lagging behind if they are not building a software park, regardless of the suitability of local conditions. As observed by Saxenian, 'Political advancement in China's new reform economy is tied closely to growth, and the decentralisation of state authority has fuelled intensifying competition between localities – particularly in the critical IT sectors.'[23] Relatively speaking, the Indian government's hands-off approach works better for a more healthy development of the software parks.

The experience of the Chinese software industry and the development of software parks suggest that the need to cultivate relationships with powerful state actors remains critical for businesses, even in regions that have aggressively adopted market mechanisms. 'Local officials in China control resources that are essential for entrepreneurs and businesses, including most notably land (which is owned by the state and controlled by local governments); and their administrative authority includes allocation of financing, infrastructure, access to licenses and permits, and the enforcement of contracts.'[24]

Multinationals in the software parks

In the Indian case, the MNCs set up their R&D centres with the aim of providing products and services to international markets. However their major purpose for entering China is to gain a foothold in the huge Chinese domestic market. These multinational corporations have forged alliances with Chinese firms in serving the local markets. On one hand they can leverage the cheap software labour costs in China and the huge market potential. On the other hand, these multinationals have brought more advanced technical skills and management expertise to the Chinese software industry, and will help advance the industry's competitiveness in the long run. In recent years, almost all the major Indian software firms have also built a presence in China, which shows the prospect of cooperation between the two countries' software firms.

With China's software capabilities becoming more sophisticated, there is a trend for the multinationals to bring their high-end R&D activities to China and India – this will be important for the improvement, and 'leapfrog' potential, of the two countries' software capabilities. According to a recent study conducted by consulting firm Booz Allen Hamilton Inc. in conjunction with the INSEAD business school, more than three-quarters of the 186 top companies surveyed have plans to build research and development sites in India and China in 2007. This eastward migration of R&D has been picking up speed for more than three decades, but has accelerated tremendously in the past few years. The study also revealed that approximately 31 per cent of R&D employees worldwide will work in India or China by the end of 2007, up from 19 per cent in 2004.[25]

Conclusions

Both India and China have a long way to go before world-class IT clusters emerge in their economies. India's main challenge is to go beyond the success of software services exports and strengthen its weakest link in the IT sector, hardware development and manufacturing. China has been strong in the hardware sector but lags far behind India in the software sector, especially in exports. Both countries face the difficult task of building on their strengths, extending them into other sectors, and fostering innovation capability in order to move up the value chain in the world market. With the rapid growth of the two most populous economies in the world, there will be explosive demand for both hardware and software domestically both in China and in India. Successful leveraging of the interrelationships between different sectors of IT, interrelationships between domestic firms and foreign multinationals will be critical to the future success of the two countries' software industries.

Further reading

Porter, M.E. (1990) *Competitive Advantage of Nations*. New York: Free Press.

Porter, M.E. (1980) *Competitive Strategy: Techniques for Analyzing Industries and Competitors*. New York: Free Press.

Notes

1. The term 'institution for collaboration' (IFC) was invented by Michael Porter, emphasising the importance of a variety of organisations that have a significant effect on competitiveness. IFCs include, for example, industry associations, professional associations, chambers of commerce, technology transfer organisations, quality centres, non-profit think tanks, university alumni associations, and others. India's NASSCOM is a good example of an IFC that has played many important roles in the course of India's software industry development.
2. For detailed discussions about these three types of software businesses, see Cusumano, M. (2004). *The Business of Software: What Every Manager, Programmer, and Entrepreneur Must Know to Thrive and Survive in Good Times and Bad*. New York: Free Press; chapter 2.
3. Porter, M.E. (ed.) (1986) *Competition in Global Industries*. Boston, MA: Harvard Business School Press; pp. 18–19.
4. Wall Street Journal (2006) 'Chinese firms seek to expand overseas', *Wall Street Journal Asian Edition*, April 5.
5. Cusumano, op. cit., p. 54.

6. Porter, M.E. (1985) *Competitive Advantage: Creating and Sustaining Superior Performance.* New York: Free Press; p. 337.
7. Ibid, pp. 321–22.
8. Saxenian, A.L. (2001) 'Bangalore: the Silicon Valley of Asia?' Center for Research on Economic Development and Policy working paper 91, 2001, 6–7.
9. Porter (1985) op. cit., p. 321.
10. Porter (1985) op. cit., p. 352.
11. 'The Intel Corporation', HBS case #9-797-137. Boston, MA: Harvard Business School Publishing; p. 8.
12. 'The Future of Enterprise Software', available at *http://www.aaccenture.com*
13. Saxenian, A.L. (2003) 'Government and Guanxi: the Chinese software industry in transition', CNEM working paper: 19.
14. Khanna, T. and Palepu, K. (1997) 'Why focused strategies may be wrong for emerging markets', *Harvard Business Review* July–August.
15. Porter, M. (2000) *On Competition.* Boston, MA: Harvard Business School Press; p. 199.
16. Saxenian (2001) op. cit.: 21.
17. This section is based on the information in Basant, R. (2006) 'Bangalore cluster: evolution, growth and challenge', Indian Institute of Management working paper 2006–05–02, and Saxenian (2001) op. cit.
18. Sen (1994) p. 55, quoted from Saxenian (2001) op. cit.: 6.
19. Saxenian (2001) op. cit.: 8.
20. Basant, op. cit.: 9.
21. This section is based on information available on the software park websites and the author's own interviews with the Dalian Software Park Cooperation.
22. By 2004, the number of software industry bases covered by the Torch Project had increased to 29.
23. Saxenian (2003) op. cit: 4.
24. Ibid.
25. Wall Street Journal (2006) 'China and India Lure Corporate Research Centers', *Wall Street Journal Asian Edition*, July 13.

7

Competitive position strategy

Introduction

Following the PESTEL and SWOT analyses of the Chinese and Indian software industries, respectively, this chapter discusses their competitive positioning strategies in the context of the global software industry. Obviously, the structure and dynamics of the Chinese software industry are different to that of the software industry in India. Moreover, the Chinese and the Indian software industries have followed different evolutionary trajectories. Interestingly, however, the software industries in both China and India are now addressing the same target market as the global opportunities cut across geographies and market segments, although the Indian software industry enjoys a first-mover advantage in the international services market. Naturally, therefore, the competitive positioning strategy of the Chinese software industry will be different to that of the Indian software industry based on the competitive scenario it faces.

This chapter presents the competitive positioning strategies for the Chinese and Indian software industries, respectively, and discusses how they can achieve and sustain global competitiveness in the software arena. It must be noted that the strategies presented here are at the industry level, and hence are collective in nature. Company-level strategies for Indian and Chinese software companies are not the focus of the discussion here, although a company-level competitive positioning strategy can be evolved in a guided manner based on the industry-level competitive positioning strategies. Drawing on the overall competitive positioning strategies presented in this chapter, Chapter 9 discusses marketing and customer-oriented strategies specific to the Chinese and Indian software industries. It also offers implications for customers as well as the other nations wishing to emulate these countries.

Competitive position strategy for the Chinese software industry

Composition of China's software industry

In a broad sense, the software sector includes all kinds of activities in the IT industry except hardware manufacturing. Software purchased from outside a company is split approximately half and half between customised professional services and more standardised products, which themselves are split roughly equally between enterprise solutions and packaged mass-market software.[1] Developed countries tend to specialise in products and higher-end services. In the past several decades, India has emerged as a role model for a developing country to achieve success in exporting software services.

Although much smaller than the IT hardware sector, China's software industry has been growing much more rapidly and reached a revenue of 390 billion RMB (approximately $49 billion) in 2005, a 40.3 per cent increase from the previous year. China's share of the world's software market was 3.55 per cent in 2005. In addition, China had over 25 software companies with annual revenues exceeding 1 billion RMB (approximately $125 million) in 2005. By category, 53 per cent of the revenue came from products sales, 34.1 per cent from system integration and 10.9 per cent from services. The export income was $3.59 billion.[2] Table 7.1 describes changes in the compositions of China's software revenues from 2004 to 2005. These figures contrast vividly with the structure of the Indian software industry: China is domestically oriented and product focused, while India is export oriented and service focused.

Most of the software purchases in China have been in the low-end applications (e.g. accounting and financial management software) market segment, which domestic suppliers dominate. However, as more

Table 7.1 Changes in the composition of China's software revenues from 2004 to 2005

	2004	2005	Change
Software products	55%	53%	−2%
System integration	34.1%	34.1%	0
Software service	10.9%	12.9%	+2%

Source: compiled from the website of the China Software Industry Association (http://www.csia.org.cn/).

Chinese consumers and businesses become exposed to international technology trends, China's demands will become more sophisticated and move toward high-end applications (e.g. enterprise resource planning, customer relationship management, and supply-chain management software) that foreign firms currently control. Other segments that have piqued the interest of Chinese end-users include IT security solutions, the Linux operating system, and applications developed for the Linux open source platform.[3]

Positioning China's software industry: which segment(s) to focus on?[4]

Heeks[5] provides a framework for understanding a nation's software industry positioning strategy: two dimensions, the target market served (domestic vs. export) and the types of business intended (service vs. packages). As illustrated in Figure 8.1, five positions, A through E are delineated. Positions A and B represent export-oriented strategies. These two positions appear more attractive to countries with cheap labour. India has developed the best model for success in position A, and Israel has been successful in position B. Today, India is a leading destination for offshore software development and IT services, accounting for nearly 60 per cent of the global offshore software and IT services market as well as approximately 50 per cent of the global BPO industry. Israel is emerging as a source of entrepreneurial firms developing software products in areas such as security and antivirus technology. In 1997, there were approximately 300 software firms in Israel, employing nearly 10,000 people, with a total revenue of more than US$1.5 billion. A large fraction of the firms are engaged in developing software packages, often technically highly sophisticated, for export markets.[6]

Position C is termed 'a third world Microsoft' with a question mark according to Heeks. Enterprises in developing countries targeting position C often suffer from formidable competition from strong international rivals. Pirate packages also pervade most markets in developing countries. Thus the domestic package strategy represented by C may not be a viable strategy for most developing countries.

Position D focuses on the domestic software services markets. As pointed out in Heeks, the vast majority of firms in developing countries occupy this market segment largely because it is by far the easiest to enter. Position D can also be a good starting point for progressing into exports. A sizeable and demanding domestic market could be the springboard from which to launch into the export market by providing a base of relevant skills, experiences, and user feedback on products and track records. In addition, a sizeable domestic market will draw large numbers of IT multinationals into collaborative relationships with local partners to serve that market. As these relationships deepen, an export component often emerges.

Position E in Figure 7.1 represents the other main success story of developing country software, with a theme of specialisation for niche markets that include sectoral niches (banking, insurance, heath administration, hotel management, mining and forestry, etc.), application niches (web browsers, add-ons or text-retrieval utilities), and linguistic niches for regional languages.

Building on the previous chapters, which addressed the business environment and the characteristics of China's software industry, next we will analyse the current status and the potential of China's software industry development in all these positions.

The domestic services market

According to CCID Consulting, the domestic IT services market grew 26 per cent in 2003, reaching nearly $7 billion. The fastest growing area is in network services. Traditionally, Chinese firms have been cautious

Figure 7.1 Strategic positioning for developing country software enterprises

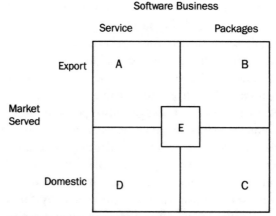

Source: Heeks, R. (1999) 'Software Strategies in Developing Countries', Working paper, Development Informatics.

about outsourcing IT services, but as firms become more focused on their own core business activities, they are becoming more willing to purchase IT services.

Implementation services represent the largest proportion of IT services market in China, followed by operations management services. In 2002, implementation services reached nearly $1.8 billion, which represents 38 per cent of the total IT-services market. By 2007, this segment will exceed $5.5 billion and account for 47 per cent of the total market. While IT services represent a relatively small portion of the total IT market compared to hardware, this segment is expected to grow substantially as the notion of procuring IT services becomes more widely accepted in China.

Local companies, such as Digital China and Legend, control the IT services market in China. In 2002, eight Chinese companies were among the top ten IT services providers. Their established sales networks among banks, manufacturers, and government agencies for computer hardware helped strengthen their client base for IT services. IBM, Hewlett-Packard, and EDS are among the major foreign players in this market segment.

It can be expected that China's rapid economic development and the ongoing massive e-commerce and e-government projects will continue to drive the growth of this market segment and create more opportunities for domestic and foreign software firms as well.

The domestic products market

On the supply side, most domestic software developers have focused on developing low-end applications software (e.g. accounting and financial management software), where they have captured 90 per cent of the market. Local companies have been able to control the market with niche applications, such as accounting software, because accounting methods in China differ from other parts of the world. They are able to provide the best and most appropriate solutions for consumers in this functional area. Foreign software companies continue to control the high-end market, such as the customer relationship management (CRM) and supply chain management (SCM) segments. Companies such as SAP (Germany) and Oracle (United States) maintain a strong presence in the market because their complete product lines allow customers to not only manage their financial systems centrally, but also manage their supply chain and plan future production.

In 2000, the top 10 firms in the Chinese packaged software market accounted for 28 per cent of total revenues, compared to 1999 when the top ten firms accounted for 35 per cent. UFsoft and Kingdee were the only domestic software companies ranked in the top 10. This reflects their dominance of the financial software market – the two firms accounted for approximately 60 per cent of China's accounting software market – and increasingly the market for enterprise resource management software. This is due primarily to their privileged knowledge of Chinese financial and managerial practices. By 2002, UFsoft had moved from 7th to 4th ranked in total package software sales, following only IBM, Microsoft, and Oracle.[7]

According to CCID Consulting, the platform software market reached 8.6 billion RMB in 2001 (approximately $1 billion). The open source platform movement has caught the attention of Chinese government leaders in the past few years.[8] IDC predicts that client-based Linux usage will grow 39 per cent, compared to 11 per cent for Windows usage, and server-based Linux usage will grow 41 per cent annually compared to only 8 per cent for Windows servers. Authorities have found the Linux open source model appealing compared to proprietary software such as that marketed by Microsoft and other Unix suppliers because it allows them to monitor what computer users are doing more closely, and the source code is free. In addition, because the source code can be viewed and further developed by anyone, authorities also believe that Linux applications could more quickly help spur on the growth of a more sophisticated domestic software industry and enhance the development of China's own operating system.

As a result, the Ministry of Information Industry and the Chinese Academy of Sciences have invested in a Linux-based software distribution company, named Red Flag Linux. As an effort to widely distribute Linux throughout the country, Red Flag Linux will donate huge volumes of the Linux operating systems to schools throughout China. Despite the popularity of the open source model among government authorities in China, Microsoft's Windows operating systems will continue to maintain the dominant share in the platform market due to their user-friendliness and the variety of Chinese-language applications developed for them. In addition, China's rampant piracy problems will prevent the widespread use of Linux. Experts estimate that 90 per cent of Windows operating systems are unlicensed copies that sell for less than one dollar on the black market. Microsoft has recognised the Chinese government's interest in the open source platform, and during Microsoft Chairman Bill Gates' meeting with President Jiang Zemin in late February 2003 he agreed to provide the Chinese government access to the Windows source code. On February 28, 2003, China's Information Technology Security Certification Center signed an agreement with Microsoft to participate in the company's Government Security Program. This program permits government officials to receive controlled access to the Windows source code and other technical information to address their national security concerns.

International products market

This market segment is almost non-existent in China's software industry. The majority of software programming in China is for the outsourcing and domestic services segment, which tends to be in the lower end of the software industry value chain. China currently lacks an entrepreneurial environment that fosters innovation. Software programming and development require imagination as well as business intuition. The product life cycle of software is so short that, in order to beat the competitor to the marketplace and fulfil the needs of the consumers, innovative software developers are increasingly required for suppliers to effectively survive in the software market. The quality of China's software developers is not comparable to that of professionals in more mature software markets. Only a few domestic software companies have received the capability maturity model (CMM) certification, which is an internationally accepted standard for assessing the level and quality of software development processes. There are a few success stories of Chinese products in the world market such as the Founder Group Corporation, which now controls 80 per cent of China's desktop publishing system market and is a dominant supplier to Overseas Chinese newspapers. Founder is a good example of leveraging success in a domestic market and finding and dominating a niche in the international market. However this type of success story is the exception rather than the rule for China's software industry.

Even though China has established several software colleges and software bases to encourage innovation, encouraged universities to develop software training programs, and provided tax and investment incentives for software development, it still remains to be seen whether training programs will effectively foster the entrepreneurial spirit seen in the 'Silicon Valleys' of the world and enable China's software firms to enter the international software products segment.

International services market

China is increasingly becoming known for software outsourcing. India, the second largest software exporting country after the United States, is watching the development of the Chinese software industry very closely to gauge how soon China will become a significant threat to India's own industry. In order to find answers to the question 'will China be a major competitor to India in the world software services market?', in 2002, NASSCOM vice president Sunil Mehta spent 15 days visiting five cities in China including Beijing, Xi'an, Dalian, Shanghai, and Shenzhen. He commissioned an independent survey of China's hardware and software market and met with government officials and private companies including software, finance, real estate, and placement firms. The basic conclusion was that 'there is no potential threat or competition from China to India in the global software market in the near future, and Indian companies could look at China as a potential market rather than a competitor'.[9]

Attempting to duplicate the Bangalore software development model, China has established several software parks with the intention of making these parks the bases for software export. Realising that China does not have the capability to compete with India for the US and European software outsourcing markets, China is now shifting its attention to the Japanese markets. Some Chinese software firms have even started to acquire Japanese software firms in order to gain deeper footholds in the Japanese markets. Recently, China's Langchao Group, one of the leading software outsourcing companies, acquired the Japanese software services provider Shinwa in an attempt to strengthen its market presence in Japan. Shinwa has strong experience in software development and marketing capabilities in areas of development of embedded software and large-scale application software development in such industries as transportation, finance, manufacturing and education.

One major obstacle for the further expansion of this market segment is the shortage of qualified human capital. First, the English capability of the Chinese software personnel is not good enough, which is a problem in services that require frequent communication with overseas offices. Second, few Chinese engineering and computer graduates are as good as their qualifications suggest. While they often have a more solid grasp of theory than their European counterparts, few leave university able to apply it to real-life problems, such as developing software. One reason is a lack of vocational training and few links between business and academia. In Europe and India, by contrast, engineering degrees demand work experience, whereas in China university teachers educated in a rigid, theory-based system are not able to prepare students for the real world. Meanwhile fears about piracy of intellectual property – more rampant in China than India – will constrain growth. Though foreign companies in China say that copying sophisticated IT processes is difficult and can be thwarted by relatively simple safeguards, the perception that sensitive business information is at risk is likely to slow development. All this suggests that, for the moment at least, China is likely to capture an increasing share of low-level BPO tasks, such as data entry, form processing and software testing, while India continues to dominate higher-value functions, such as research and design, which require greater creativity and language skills. However, this will change as more western firms demand support in China and domestic opportunities grow. And it isn't just pure competition between the two countries: last year, TCS signed a deal with the Chinese government and Microsoft to build China's first big software company, which aims to provide IT services for the Olympics.[10]

Based on the above analysis of the four market segments: international services, international products, domestic services and domestic products, we may conclude that although it is predictable that there will be Chinese star firms emerging in all these market segments, at the overall industry level China should focus on its domestic markets as a starting point and develop a more comprehensive development strategy in the long term.

Competitive position strategy for the Indian software industry

As depicted in Figure 7.2, the Indian software industry has a substantial competitive scope, spanning products, services and consulting opportunities across the globe. With many emerging markets, a growing domestic market, and with expanding global IT spends, the opportunities available to the Indian software industry are really compelling. However, the competition in the global software and IT industry is also intensifying, and this means that the Indian software industry must approach the market with a portfolio of competitive strategies in order to gain a stronger foothold in the global software industry landscape and establish its supremacy. The next sections briefly discuss the competitive scenario faced by the Indian software industry and competitive positioning strategies it can adopt to achieve competitiveness in the global marketplace.

Figure 7.2	Opportunity scope for the Indian software industry

COMPETITIVE SCOPE

Software & IT Services	Solutions	Consulting	Products
Application Development, Maintenance, Reengineering, BPO, KPO, Infrastructure Management, Testing, R&D and Engineering Services	IT-based Business Solutions e.g., Supply Chain Optimisation	IT Strategy, Architecture Consulting, Process Consulting	Mass Market Products Enterprise Products

Competitive analysis of the Indian software industry

National competitiveness in a specific industry depends on a host of factors including vision and strategy, global demand, international linkages and trade situations, industry clusters, input factors, and perceptions of trust and credibility. The Indian software industry, which has largely been an export-oriented software and IT services industry, has recorded an impressive CAGR of approximately 40 per cent over the last decade. It has gained prominence on the world map because of its low-cost, high-quality software development and delivery capability, and has emerged as the most preferred offshore destination for software work. The Indian software firms have so far succeeded by adopting the strategy of cost leadership. In recent times, a large number of MNCs have also established their software operations in India, while other software nations have emerged on the scene. As a result, the competitive landscape has changed dramatically, requiring the Indian software firms to discover new sources of differentiation, engage in diversification, and target newer segments in addition to sustaining cost leadership.

Based on Porter's five forces framework, Figure 7.3 captures the competitive scenario for the Indian software industry.

As the figure suggests, clearly there is an intensification of competition, especially in the software and IT service space, because of new entrants such as the Philippines, Vietnam, China, Brazil, Russia, Mexico, and some Eastern European nations such as the Czech Republic and Poland. Emergence of these players obviously means that the customers now have more choices and thus more bargaining power, particularly in the low-value services sector. This means that the market for application development, maintenance, infrastructure services, business process outsourcing and the like will increasingly be price sensitive. While from a customer confidence point of view, the Indian

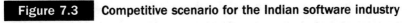

Figure 7.3   Competitive scenario for the Indian software industry

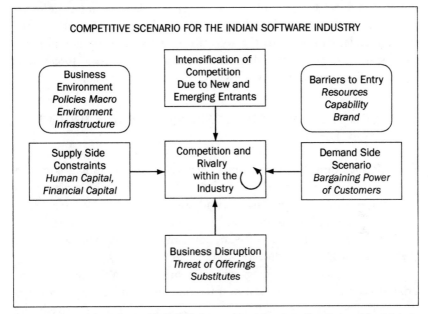

Source: adapted from Porter, M. (1985) *Competitive Advantage: Creating and Sustaining Superior Performance*. New York: Free Press.

software industry continues to have an edge over the other players because of its supremacy in quality processes and performance track record, growing competition from other low-cost countries and wage inflation within the Indian software industry is likely to place the profit margins of Indian software firms under pressure. The competition within the industry could also potentially catalyse a destructive price war and affect profitability. Likewise, if the Indian software industry continues to be a predominantly services-focused industry and does not diversify into products, then the scarcity of factor inputs such as human capital could affect its competitiveness. Lack of high-quality infrastructure is another factor that could impede industry growth.

However, there are lucrative opportunities for the Indian software industry in products, high-value consulting, and high-margin business solutions segments that it must strategically target to secure new growth platforms, while focusing on differentiating the traditional software and IT services. This means that the industry needs to diversify to explore newer segments both domestically and in international markets, although it will have to deal with issues related to resources and capabilities, understanding of markets, brand, local regulations, credibility and board-level relationships in the case of consulting and the like, and some of those issues could be barriers to entry for the Indian software industry. However, the threat of substitutes, either in terms of offerings or in terms of large-scale disruption to the software services industry, is really not imminent, suggesting that there are basically four major forces that influence the competitiveness of the Indian software industry.

Competitive position strategies for the Indian software industry

Formulating competitive positioning strategies for the Indian software industry is somewhat tricky because it includes not only firms incorporated in India but also subsidiaries of MNCs. However, as a deliberate choice, the competitive positioning strategies discussed here apply primarily to *Indian* software companies, although good part of them would also be relevant to MNCs.

The competitive positioning strategies presented here are organised around geographical (domestic and international) and market segments (products and services), although it is also possible to approach the development of competitive strategies around industry segments (defence, e-business, etc.) or around established and emerging markets. Finally, the competitive positioning strategies discussed here are based on the assumption that the sustainability of a profitable software industry depends on pursuing both products and services businesses[11] in a balanced manner and strategically exploiting complementarities between them.

Figure 7.4 captures the competitive positioning strategies for the Indian software industry. These positioning strategies have been organised around two broad geographic segments, namely domestic and international, and two broad market/business segments, namely products and services. The competitive positioning strategies have been developed using Porter's competitive advantage framework[12], which suggests *cost leadership*, *differentiation* and *focus* as three distinct competitive strategies. Also, this strategy formulation relies upon *scaling*, *duplication* and *granulation* as three growth strategies as suggested by von Krogh and Cusumano.[13] The discussion of competitive positioning strategies here also integrates competitiveness levers such as 'value disciplines',[14] globalisation, diversification, alliances, and acquisitions. In the following, competitive positioning strategies for each of the four identified segments are presented.

Figure 7.4	Competitive position strategies for the Indian software industry

Competitive Strategies	Growth Strategies	Competitiveness Levers
• Cost leadership • Differentiation • Focus	• Scaling • Duplication • Granulation	• 'Value Disciplines' • Alliances & Partnerships • Diversification • Globalisation • Mergers & Acquisitions

International (Services)

Application development and maintenance, reengineering, application integration, package implementation, infrastructure management services, independent verification & validation services, R&D and engineering services
Strategic Positioning: Cost leadership + differentiation, duplication and value disciplines; scaling through globalisation and acquisitions for vertical capability, thought leadership

Business and Knowledge Process Outsourcing
Strategic Positioning: Cost leadership, value disciplines

Large, complex, integrated outsourcing deals
Strategic Positioning: Cost leadership + differentiation, value disciplines; trusted partner positioning with focus on business transformation

Vertical Business Solutions
Strategic Positioning: Cost leadership + differentiation, exploit partnerships and alliances, thought leadership

Small and medium enterprises
Opportunities: Software as Service, Hosted Services
Strategic Positioning: Cost leadership, duplication

International (Products)

Application products (e.g. retail and corporate banking), communication software products (mobile/wireless communication), IP licensing (semiconductor, media & entertainment, DSP, mobility)
Strategic Positioning: Cost leadership + differentiation; fast follower strategy

Diversification into vertical specific products, products for niche markets, disruptive products (e.g. communications, security), products for digital markets
Strategic Positioning: Cost leadership + differentiation, R&D focus, IPR ownership; fast follower strategy

Emerging products for emerging markets; low-cost products for developing economies
Strategic Positioning: cost leadership + differentiation; joint ventures (e.g. in China); cost leadership + imitation

Domestic (Services)

Application Development, Consulting, Business Solutions and IT Infrastructure Services for Large Corporations
Key Verticals: Banking and Finance, Retail, Telecoms, Automotive, Pharmaceuticals and Manufacturing. Also, defence sector
Strategic Positioning: Cost leadership + differentiation, duplication, and value disciplines

Business and Knowledge Process Outsourcing
Key Verticals: Banking, Pharmaceuticals, Retail
Strategic Positioning: Cost leadership, value disciplines, and duplication

Education services, Internet applications services, mobile telephony value added services
Strategic Positioning: Cost leadership, focus, granulation, acquisitions

Small and medium enterprises
Opportunities: Software as Service, Hosted Services, Consulting Strategic Positioning: Cost leadership, duplication

Domestic (Products)

Application products (e.g. retail and corporate banking), communication software products (mobile/wireless communication), consumer electronics, media and entertainment products, healthcare and medical electronics products, packages/products for retail, pharmaceutical and banking sectors (e.g. low-cost ATM), open source software products for mass markets
Strategic Positioning: Cost leadership + differentiation; cost leadership + imitation; licensing agreements, R&D focus, and joint R&D with international players/partners/alliances

Software and IT products for the defence sector
Strategic Positioning: Cost leadership, imitation

International services market

India has traditionally focused on the international services market, which is large and growing. In addition to the traditional software services opportunities such as application development, maintenance and reengineering services, there are also huge global opportunities in such areas as applications integration, package implementation, infrastructure management services, and independent software verification and validation services. However, in correspondence with these opportunities, the competition the Indian software industry faces is also intensifying. The Indian software firms so far have achieved their market leadership in the services space through low-cost, high-quality performance. However, moving forward, they will need to differentiate, and exploit economies of scale as well as scope to stay competitive and grow.

Specifically, the Indian software industry will have to employ a dual strategy of cost leadership and differentiation to deliver low-cost, high-quality, on-time but differentiated services to clients. The differentiation could come from strong domain knowledge, R&D-based IP assets resulting in superior service quality and shorter time to delivery. In addition, the Indian software firms could augment their competitive positioning strategies by globalising their operations in other low-cost countries such as China, Vietnam, the Philippines, Brazil, Russia and the Czech Republic by employing the growth strategies of scaling and duplication. To strengthen their competitive posture, the Indian firms will need to selectively acquire overseas companies to gain scale, vertical capability, and proximity (including cultural proximity) to customers. In addition, the Indian software firms must continue to excel in practicing 'value disciplines', leveraging their operational excellence, customer intimacy and relationships that they have developed over the years, and superior software development and delivery performance.

The international software services market also offers growing opportunities in R&D and engineering services, and these too fall well within the competitive scope for the Indian software industry. The drivers for the outsourcing of R&D and engineering services are primarily the need to contain costs, establish focus on core competencies, leverage new capabilities and achieve flexibility. The Indian software industry can compete effectively in the R&D and engineering services market leveraging its cost leadership, availability of a strong technical resource pool, and by leveraging its proven offshore delivery model. As typically the Indian software firms also serve their clients' clients, they can capitalise on this unique position to provide valuable insights to the technology companies they serve by providing a two-way feedback loop.

The Indian software industry, having already taken a lead in the business and knowledge process outsourcing space, has huge opportunities ahead of it in the growing global BPO and KPO segment. The global BPO and KPO markets are fast growing, and India is advantageously positioned to capitalise on the opportunities in this segment. A large English-speaking resource pool and operational excellence are in favour of the Indian software and IT services industry. Members of the higher-level skills pool required for the KPO segment such as equity research, patent searching and drafting, bioinformatics, etc. are available in large numbers in India. As its competitive positioning strategy for this segment, the Indian software industry should combine cost leadership with deep domain knowledge, and leverage customer relationships that firms have developed to grow its foothold in this segment. Operational excellence will be vital to sustain healthy margins in this segment. A winning competitive positioning would involve positioning the Indian software industry as a provider of integrated software and BPO services. In addition, BPO operations in other low-cost nations to serve non-English speaking customers would be a vital element of the overall strategy, which will need to be operationalised through global expansion or acquisitions.

The market for technology-based business solutions is very lucrative and offers a natural value migration path for the Indian software industry. Increasingly, firms the world over are looking at harnessing technology to address their competitive needs. Technology-based business solutions (e.g. supply chain optimisation, infrastructure consolidation and virtualisation, mobile sales force automation, real-time analytics, etc.) offer tremendous promise. To profitably address this market segment, Indian software firms will need to position themselves with a strategic convergence of cost leadership and differentiation in addition to acquiring deep domain skills to operate in the vertical solutions market. Differentiation will come by investing in performing business relevant R&D, and exploiting partnerships and alliances with leading technology platform vendors. Low-cost, high-performance systems integration capability will be necessary for success in the solutions space. Moreover, the ability to demonstrate thought leadership will be vital. The current inadequacy of domain skills could be strategically compensated for by co-opting leading customers in the solution definition and development process. In addition, Indian firms should adopt a granulation strategy for the solutions segment to focus on those verticals such as banking and finance, insurance, and retail where there are not only large market opportunities but also an accumulation of experiential knowledge gained through providing software services.

The small- and medium-enterprises segment in the international software services market is an area that offers huge potential for the Indian software industry, although the nuances of this segment mean it has unique requirements. First of all, business in this segment could drive its operational efficiency and competitiveness through IT but is usually constrained in making the requisite investments. This also means this segment is price sensitive. Indian software firms can strategically position themselves to compete in this area by leveraging cost leadership and operational excellence, and offer software as service, hosted services, and IT planning services, besides low-cost software solutions and services. Adopting the strategy of duplication, which would allow Indian software firms to capitalise on their knowledge, experiences, and capabilities acquired through serving the large, diverse firms, will ensure a competitive edge for the Indian industry in the SME segment.

International products market

The international products market scene is currently dominated by a few large players such as Microsoft, IBM, Oracle, SAP, Symantec, EMC, Computer Associates and Adobe, and some niche players such as McAfee. The products market has witnessed a trend towards consolidation, with a few major acquisitions in the last two years. So, a competitive analysis of the global software industry suggests that entering the software products market, especially in the areas of enterprise and mass-market products, will be quite challenging, particularly in the wake of increasing consolidation and deep entrenchment of the established players. A software firm interested in pursuing a products business would therefore need to craft a strategy that either leads to considerable differentiation or market disruptions, or focus on niche-product markets.

There are several opportunities that the Indian software industry can address to enlarge its competitive span and market penetration. For example, there are attractive opportunities to develop applications products for sectors such as banking, telecoms and retail. Many Indian companies are already active in the software products space, with growing international market share. Leading examples include Finacle and Flexcube, banking products from Infosys Technologies and i-flex Solutions, respectively; Marshall, an ERP package from Ramco Systems;

and telecom products from Subex Systems. However, India's footprint in the global software products space is rather small, although the leading Indian product vendors recorded an average growth of 36 per cent in the fiscal year 2004–2005.

Low total cost of ownership (TCO) has emerged as a key success factor for software products, and this means that Indian software firms can achieve a competitive positioning through cost leadership while simultaneously focusing on differentiating their products to gain a foothold in the international markets. Product operations based in India benefit not only from lower development costs but also low cost of support, thus lowering the TCO. Besides application products, there are also considerable market opportunities in areas such as communication software products in the wireless and mobility space as well as in the media and entertainment space, including gaming software.

In order to pursue the highly competitive international products market, the Indian firms will need to employ a combination of cost leadership and focus. In addition, fast-follower and imitation strategies would also augment their competitive positioning. The emerging markets present attractive opportunities for developing low-cost, innovative products, and Indian firms can approach these opportunities by setting up joint ventures, for example with China. However, besides low-cost products for the emerging markets, this segment offers opportunities for introducing disruptive product innovations in areas such as digital media, communications, and security.

The global innovation ecosystem also presents a compelling opportunity for Indian software houses to diversify into IP licensing. The market is replete with opportunities in the areas of semiconductors, media and entertainment, digital signal processing (DSP), and wireless communications. Pursuing such markets will require Indian software firms to establish a focus on specific segments and leverage cost leadership. There are already a few Indian companies such as Ittiam Systems, ImpulseSoft, and Sasken that are active in the IP licensing arena, and they are growing handsomely.

Pursuing opportunities in the international products segment, however, has certain investment implications for Indian software firms. Competitive positioning strategies for the international products market will require an R&D focus and investments in brand building. While some of the required R&D investments can be lowered by strategically adopting imitation, establishing a brand for the Indian software products will indeed need investment and substantial marketing efforts. In addition, Indian software firms will need to invest in building a culture for innovation and the ability to manage risks. This also means that they will need to learn to organise and manage projects differently to those in the controlled, process-driven environments – an approach that has been the foundation for sustained growth in the international services market.

Domestic services market

The last three to four years have seen a real boom in the Indian economy and a significant growth in such sectors as banking and finance, retail, telecoms, automotive, manufacturing, and pharmaceuticals. Competitiveness in these sectors has meant strategic adoption of IT and, as a result, the overall IT spend in the country has grown substantially. Due to the sheer size of the Indian market and growth opportunities, IT projects in sectors such as retail, telecoms, banking, and energy and utilities are typically very large and complex. This presents a huge business opportunity for Indian software services firms, which have hitherto not really been active in the domestic services segment. As in the international services segment, the large domestic corporations have a heavy appetite for consuming traditional IT services such as applications development and maintenance, and infrastructure management. In addition, there are equally compelling opportunities for consulting and business solutions. However, the global IT services players such as IBM and HP are also very active in the Indian services market, and often they serve their customers using their low-cost resource base in India.

The Indian software and IT services market is quite price sensitive, so Indian software firms will need to competitively position themselves using the dual strategy of cost leadership and differentiation, providing low-cost, differentiated services and solutions. They also will need to employ duplication as a growth strategy, which will allow them to duplicate their success in the export market and gain a competitive edge in the domestic market by leveraging their superior process capabilities and the domain skills they have acquired by serving international clients. Whilst their operational excellence will be to their advantage, Indian firms will need to acquire customer intimacy and deliver superior performance by understanding the local customer and market nuances and handling domestic customer idiosyncrasies. Indian software firms can also capitalise on growing domestic BPO opportunities by competitively positioning themselves through the strategy of cost leadership. Their operational capability and experiences gained in serving the international clients would lend them strength in pursuing the domestic BPO market segment. Similar to the international SME segment, Indian software firms also have opportunities in the domestic SME segment. Prima facie, there is no striking difference between the SME segments in the international market and the domestic market, except that Indian SMEs are likely to be more price sensitive. Therefore, as in the case of the international SME services segment, the competitive positioning strategies for the Indian SME segment will also warrant cost leadership and operational excellence, and a focus on offering software as service, hosted services, IT planning services, and low-cost IT solutions.

The rapid growth in the Indian economy and the increasing penetration of the Internet and mobile telephony offer enormous opportunities for Indian firms in such areas as Internet application services, Internet-based communication services, value added mobile application services, and educational services delivered over the Internet and broadband networks. The competition in these opportunity segments is currently relatively low and the markets are in their embryonic stages. This means that there are good growth prospects for Indian firms, and in particular entrepreneurial ventures, in these segments. Therefore, firms that have value-added offerings are likely to gain from opportunities in these segments. With the Indian market being price sensitive, however, cost leadership must serve as the strategic backbone for competitive success in these domestic segments. Large firms that are looking to diversify and capitalise on these market opportunities could acquire niche, small, entrepreneurial companies to drive their competitive positioning.

Domestic products market

The market for software products is growing at a fast pace in India owing to the overall economic boom, increasing computer density, rising penetration of the Internet, and significant IT spend by the corporate and educational sectors. The markets for enterprise and mass-market products are currently dominated by companies such as Microsoft, Adobe, Autodesk, IBM, Sun Microsystems, SAP, Oracle, and Symantec. However, quite like the international products market, the domestic products market segment in India also presents attractive opportunities for application products such as banking applications and vertical-specific packages for sectors such as retail, and automotive. Banking products by Indian firms such as Infosys Technologies (Finacle) and i-flex Solutions (Flexcube) have already been adopted by many banks in India.

Tally, an accounting package, enjoys a substantial market presence in India. However, the Indian software products market is quite price sensitive and, moreover, the companies also have to deal with the risk of piracy. A sustainable competitive positioning strategy for the Indian software products market segment would therefore involve convergence of cost leadership and differentiation.

The domestic product market also offers opportunities for developing low-cost products for wireless and mobile communications, digital media and entertainment and supply-chain management aligned to the emerging market context. The opportunity to develop mass-market and enterprise software products, especially for small and medium enterprises, using open source software, is also very compelling. In addition, there are niche vertical segments such as pharmaceuticals (knowledge and data management), education (content delivery, collaboration and interaction platforms) and healthcare (software/IT based patient monitoring, diagnostics and treatment delivery solutions) that will be very receptive to low-cost products suited to the Indian context. The Indian defence sector also offers huge prospects and will welcome indigenous, low-cost high-quality products relevant to its need.

The competitive positioning to pursue these opportunities will require firms to focus on niche market segments in addition to employing the strategy of cost leadership. Investments in R&D and capital to fund entrepreneurial ventures would be required. Indian firms pursuing these markets could employ the strategy of imitation as part of their competitive positioning strategies. Indian firms exploring the domestic products market segment could also licence technologies, or enter into joint R&D agreements with their international partners, or set-up joint ventures with foreign product firms to develop and adapt products for the Indian market. Of course, a well-crafted marketing and branding strategy would be vital for competitive success.

The opportunities available to the Indian software industry are enormous, both in the international and domestic segments. The competitive positioning strategies for the services sector will obviously be different to those of the products sector. Similarly, the characteristics of the competitive positioning strategies for the domestic market segments will vary when compared to those for the international market segments. Moreover, it must be recognised that while a combination of competitive strategies, growth strategies and competitiveness levers do apply for each market segment, the competitive positioning strategies are likely to be dynamic in nature depending on the evolving market contexts. Therefore, the competitiveness of the Indian firms will rely on their ability to be adaptive and strategically leverage their resources, capabilities, scale, and relationship capital for global dominance.

Conclusions

This chapter has discussed the competitive positioning strategies for the Chinese and Indian software industries, respectively. As is evident, there are similarities and differences between the competitive positioning strategies for China and India. The similarities are due to the fact that both the Chinese and Indian software industries are targeting the lucrative global software services exports markets, whereas the differences stem from the contextual and structural differences that characterise the Chinese and Indian software industries. The next chapter discusses specific customer and market oriented strategies China and India can adopt in order to secure their competitiveness and growth.

Further reading

Readers interested in an in-depth analysis of the competitiveness issues in the software industry may refer to Hoch, D.J., et al (2000) *Secrets of Software Success* (Harvard Business School Press), that offers insights on success drivers in the software industry based on a study of hundred software firms around the globe. *Software Ecosystem: Understanding an Indispensable Technology and Industry* by D. Messerschmitt and C. Szyperski (MIT Press, 2003) provides a holistic understanding of the software industry and its ecosystem.

Notes

1. Ghemawat, P. (2000) 'The Indian software industry at the millennium', working paper 9-700-036. Boston, MA: Harvard Business School.
2. 'Comments on China's software industry development in 2005', from the Ministry of Information Industry website. Available at *http://www.mii.gov .cn/art/2006/03/15/art_62_8308.html* (accessed 21 November 2006).
3. See *http://web.ita.doc.gov/ITI/itiHome.nsf/($All)/7D45B83A1D21DFB 485256D0C006888BE/$FILE/ExportITChina.html* (accessed 21 November 2006).

4. The following several paragraphs are quoted from Li, M. and Gao, M. (2003) 'Strategies for developing China's software industry', *Information Technology & International Development*, 1(1): 61–73.

5. Heeks, R. (1999) 'Software strategies in developing countries', working paper. Development Informatics.

6. Arora, A.V.S., Arunachalarm, J., Asundi, and Fernandes, R. (2001) 'Indian software services industry', *Research Policy*, 30:1267–87.

7. Saxenian, A.L. (2003) 'Government and Guanxi: the Chinese software industry in transition', CNEM working paper: 18.

8. Li, M, Lin, Z and Xia, M. (2005) 'Leveraging the open source software movement for development of China's software industry', *Information Technologies and International Development*, 2(2): 45–63.

9. Kumar, A. (2002) 'China no threat to Indian software in the near future'. Available at *http://www.anancialexpress.com/fe_full_story.php?content_id=5872* (April 2; accessed 21 November 2006).

10. Economist (2006) 'Outsourcing to China: watch out, India', *Economist*, May 4.

11. Cusumano, M. (2004) *The Business of Software: What Every Manager, Programmer, and Entrepreneur Must Know to Thrive and Survive in Good Times and Bad*. New York: Free Press. Michael Cusumano – a leading scholar of the international software industry – observed that successful software businesses require both products and services focus. Although his observations were meant to guide the business strategies of individual software firms, they are relevant even at the industry level (chapter co-author Deependra Moitra's analysis).

12. Porter, M.E. (1985) *Competitive Advantage: Creating and Sustaining Superior Performance*. New York: Free Press.

13. von Krogh, G. and Cusumano, M. (2001) 'Three strategies for managing fast growth', *Sloan Management Review*, Spring. *Scaling* is about doing more of what one is good at, *duplication* refers to repeating a successful business model in other regions, and *granulation* is about growing select business options with unique capabilities to create new business.

14. Treacy, M. and Wiersema, F. (1997) *The Discipline of Market Leaders*. Perseus Books. 'Value disciplines' emphasise *operational excellence, customer intimacy*, and *superior performance* as strategic approaches to sustainable market leadership.

8

Pursuing competitive strategies

Introduction

The emergence of the global software industry offers several new opportunities and threats for many firms operating in the software sector. Almost two decades ago, Daniel Schwartz (managing director of Ulmer Brothers, a New York based investment bank), was quoted as saying 'we the United States are facing more competitors worldwide, many of whom are very aggressive and don't play by the same business rules'. A global software industry not only means more competitors, it also means greater opportunity. As discussed in Chapter 1, many large computer service providers in the US earn significant revenues from their overseas operations. From a wider perspective, the global software industry introduces greater complexities with which firms have to deal with. Technological advances made in the last decade have added to these complexities and opportunities. Although some CEOs may argue this point, the West is now in direct competition with China and India, and in the future some firms will be fighting for economic survival, future markets and profits. In this global software industry, firms are also up against the complexity of dealing with different cultures, commitments and business strategies. Operating in a global industry has been a very painful experience for many European and US firms; it demands continuous innovation and significant changes in the way organisations operate and manage themselves, specifically, in the way they manage to maintain or increase their competitive advantage.[1] To achieve an advantage over their competitors many software firms in the next 5 to 10 years will have little choice but to innovate, change more and indeed change more frequently than in the last 10 years. This represents a formidable challenge for those CEOs with global profit and loss and shareholder accountabilities.

The need to evaluate strategic alternatives is a paramount prerequisite to understanding the global opposition. Firms can develop effective global strategies by systematically analysing the specific global business drivers affecting their industries and the distinctive characteristics of their product or service businesses. A major aspect in international business is the use of strategy formulation. One key theme is that strategy formulation is dependent to some degree on industry characteristics, and on specific business drivers. A second key aspect is the use of global strategy – it should be remembered that the use of global strategy differs by dimension for each element of the value chain within a given market segment. As a mechanism for analysing the competitive position of a firm's internal operations, Porter[2] introduced the value chain concept, by which every single activity within a firm's cycle of production, marketing, delivery and support can be broken down to reveal the potential for improving both cost and differentiation at an early stage. A firm gains competitive advantage by performing these strategically-important activities more cheaply or better than its competitors. The value chain links into those of its suppliers upstream and its buyers downstream, and each needs to be understood as part of the competitive process, as do the value chains of competitors. Differences among competitor value chains are a key source of competitive advantage.

In its generic form, the value chain is the flow from inbound logistics, marketing and services, with an overlaying infrastructure of procurement, technological development, human resource development, and organisation and management. When the value chain of a business unit is linked to the value chains of its suppliers and customers, a value system is defined that is similar to the total vertical marketing system. Adding competitors to the value chain will allow for the analysis of horizontal relations within the industry. Indian software firms, such as Tata Consultancy Services, have used the concept of value chains to define the firm's strategic core. The strategic core of a firm is represented by assets of high specificity that are necessary to attain the firm's strategic goals. Any such assets should be managed internally, making the full range of organisational incentives available for their control. The strategic core is generally close to the firm's business idea that sets it apart relative to other competing firms. For example, IBM uses the slogan 'The Other IBM' to differentiate its consulting business. IBM sees their business consulting service as a core asset that gives them a differential lead over other consulting and service providers.

One method of defining a firm's strategic core is to realise that time is often the critical variable in competitive success. For example, Tata Consultancy Services sees its strategic core to be its ability to cut short the 'application development phase' in medium and large software projects, and to add value through its specialist consultancy services. It could be argued that the significance of any strategic core a firm possesses within the value chain is ultimately a function of its impact on relative cost or differentiation that in turn stems from industry structure. Though a firm can have innumerable strengths and weaknesses vis-à-vis its competitors, there are two basic types of competitive advantage a firm can possess: low cost, or differentiation. The significance of any strength or weakness a firm possesses is ultimately a function of its impact on relative cost or differentiation. Cost advantage and differentiation in turn stem from industry structure.

Competitive advantage

Competitive advantage grows out of the value a firm is able to create for its buyers that exceeds the firm's cost of creating it. Value is what buyers are willing to pay, and superior value stems from offering lower prices than competitors for equivalent benefits or providing unique benefits that more than offset a higher price. There are two basic types of competitive advantage: cost leadership and differentiation. The relative position of a firm or country within the global software industry is given by its choice of competitive advantage (cost versus differentiation) and its choice of competitive scope. Figure 8.1 attempts to position China and India relative to their respective strengths and weaknesses. In essence, China is perceived to have cost advantage over India in low-cost software products, whereas India will likely be dominant in product research and development.

In addition to both China and India, numerous developing countries are striving to enter the global software industry: countries such as Russia would welcome the opportunity to be host to the next Bangalore or Silicon Valley. For many countries, the barriers to entry are difficult and many would-be players such as Malaysia and the Philippines are falling short of their intended aspirations. China has managed to gain a foothold on the international ladder through low labour costs and attractive tax incentives. Its collaboration with Hong Kong software firms has helped to focus and increase its competitive scope.

Competitive scope distinguishes between firms targeting broad industry segments (Chapter 5) and firms focusing on a narrow segment. Here, generic strategies are useful because they characterise strategic positions at the simplest and broadest level. Porter maintains that achieving competitive advantage requires a firm to make a choice about

Figure 8.1	China vs India: global generic strategies

	China v India Global Advantage	
Competitive Strategy	China future cost leadership in software products *Drivers: Investment, R&D, technology, education and training*	India future differentiation in high product technology research and development *Drivers: Economic focus, R&D and software processes*
	India future cost focus on next generation of application services *Drivers: Knowledge, Skills, Partnerships, Investment and Political Relationships*	China and India future focus on product differentiation in low–medium software application products *Drivers: Investment and R&D technology processes and joint ventures*

the type and scope of its competitive advantage, for example, India's access to skilled employees and capable suppliers. There are different risks inherent in each generic strategy, but being 'all things to all people' is a sure recipe for mediocrity – that is, getting 'stuck in the middle'. Although the options (cost leadership, differentiation, cost focus and differentiation focus) are not considered to be mutually exclusive – each requires total commitment and organisational arrangements – it is considered rare for a firm to succeed by pursuing more than one strategy at a time, and they are likely to be unsuccessful. For example, achieving cost leadership and differentiation are usually inconsistent, because differentiation is usually costly. To be unique and command a price premium, a differentiator deliberately evaluates costs. Conversely, cost leadership often requires a firm to forego some differentiation by standardising its product, reducing marketing overhead, and the like.[3]

Cost leadership

Cost leadership is a low-cost competitive strategy that aims at the broad mass market and requires offensive building of efficient scale facilities, vigorous pursuit of cost reductions from experience, tight cost overhead control, avoidance of marginal customer accounts, and cost minimisation in areas such as research and development, service sales force, and advertising, etc. According to Porter, cost leadership is perhaps the clearest of the three generic strategies. If organisations are to sustain prosperous cost leadership across their range of activities, they must be clear on how this is to be accomplished through various elements of the value chain.

Both China and India differ in cost structure and in the way they perceive the world, and in the pool of talent and ideas being generated on an ongoing basis. Understanding the comparative advantages of countries effectively and efficiently can create significant competitive advantages for a firm. As low-cost providers, China and India are in a better position to survive a price war, and an awareness of this may block higher cost competitors from competing on price. Demands from buyers to lower price are likely to be weak as customers are unlikely to be able to consistently get a better deal from the cost leader's rivals. If suppliers raise prices, the low-cost producer will not be forced to respond as much as other, higher cost competitors. The firm's low-cost position may well deter entry to the market by competitors, especially if the potential entrant hopes to compete on price. For example, India's export success has been built on its low-cost market advantage and by sustaining linkages with US markets and customers. A cost leader must achieve parity or proximity in the bases of differentiation relative to its competitors to be an above-average performer, even though it relies on cost leadership for its competitive advantage. Parity in the bases of differentiation allows a cost leader to translate its cost advantage directly into higher profits compared to those of competitors. Proximity in differentiation means that the price discount necessary to achieve an acceptable market share does not offset a cost leader's cost advantage, and hence the cost leader earns above average returns. However, there are a number drawbacks to implementing a cost leader strategy. These include:

- The risk of technological change that may increase the need for large sums of capital investment to retain position: this may cancel out all cost advantages achieved.

- The threat of competition from other countries (both China and India are under threat from countries such as Russia, Malaysia, the Philippines and Vietnam). Although Chinese firms and Chinese officials publicise their desire to become a major offshore software destination, China should not be considered to be in head-to-head competition for global outsourcing software projects as wage rates in China are already higher than those in Vietnam, China does not have the inherent advantages over Vietnam that India has (for example, natural fluency in English), and many firms utilising China cite their stake in the Chinese domestic markets as influencing their decision to develop software there.

- The threat by competitors to portion the market, or build up a high-price high-quality brand image (an overall low-cost service provider would then have to compete on cost in each market segment it operated in, and hope that cheaper prices can compete successfully against brand image).

- Labour inflation – this is always a danger, especially when competitors in other countries do not have the same rising labour costs (for example, in China, wages for workers in the software industry are very low by international standards. Chinese software workers earn around half what their Indian counterparts do; a Beijing resident computer science graduate would earn in the region of $6,500 a year).

Differentiation

The second generic strategy is aimed at the broad mass market and involves the creation of a product or service that is perceived throughout its industry as unique. It selects one or more attributes that buyers in an industry perceive as significant, and uniquely positions itself to meet those needs. It is rewarded for its uniqueness with a premium price. With a successful differentiation strategy, loyalty to the firm's products will increase, and – assuming that customers are not too price sensitive – the firm can charge premium prices for its products and services that are higher than those that could be charged by the least-cost producer in the market. Differentiation seems to offer a way forward for India – as well as developing new and differentiated services India is capitalising on its capability and ability in research and development, bringing out new products in existing markets. Moving into differentiated markets can bring many of the benefits of being a market leader. There is a school of thought that suggests that a firm that uses a strategy of differentiation will not be the market leader in terms of market share. The principal risk with a differentiation strategy is that customers will not want to pay premium prices for the different product or service. Some further implications for differentiation strategies are as follows:

- The firm must provide some distinguishing characteristic, such as superior quality. India's ability to produce fit-for-purpose software has been marked through its adoption of the internationally-recognised

Capability Maturity Model (CMM),[4] and a question mark remains over the ability of China to move from low-value services to higher-value software services. By implementing the CMM, India has increased its standing within the software industry and as thus become a more attractive proposition to US firms wishing to partner with foreign providers.

- The firm must continually seek to innovate, to stay ahead of its rivals in quality and other differentiating attributes. For example, if rivals innovate, the firm should try to imitate them quickly. Consequently, a differentiating firm will need to have a large budget to support research and development and advertising. China has already started a process of massive research and development coupled with privatisation. The list of Chinese state-owned enterprises likely to become global and prominent players includes the Peking University Group and Legend Holdings, which provides personal computers, or Huawei and Zhongxing, which develop much of their software internally for the telecommunications and associated markets.

It is worth noting that 'price' does not always need to faithfully track differentiation; it can also play an independent role in fine-tuning a competitive strategy. A positively-differentiated offering can be sold at a premium price; however, the seller is not obliged to charge the whole or any of those premiums. In some cases, it may be advantageous to charge less than the full premium and thereby invest in extra market share by sacrificing short-term profits. Such gains in share may lead to scale economies and consequently longer-term advantages. The investment in market share by keener pricing is less often available in the limiting case of commodity-buy strategy. As for all investment, the one in market share incurs competitive risks: competitors may respond by price cuts of their own or with innovations that leapfrog and displace the seller's offering, thereby devaluing its investment.

Focus

The focus strategy involves the selection of a market segment or group of segments in the industry, and meeting the needs of that preferred segment (or niche) better than the other market competitors. Focus strategies can be either cost or differentiation focused. Both variants of the focus strategy rest on differences between target segments. For example, the Chinese firm UFSoft[5] (founded in 1993) has its own unique accounting and market brands. Its success is attributed to the type of accounting software it produces – the accounting system in China is unique, and it is hard for foreign firms to compete. Cost focus takes advantage of differences in the cost behaviour in some segments, (a cost focus strategy does necessitate that a trade-off between profitability and overall market share to be made), while differentiation focus exploits the special needs of buyers in certain segments such as luxury goods. As for the other two generic strategies, there are a few risks to adopting the focus strategy. These are:

- the market segment may not be large enough to provide profits for the firm and its shareholders;
- the segments needs may eventually become less distinct from the main market;
- competition may move in and take over the chosen market segment – this is clearly an issue for India in that India is reliant on service exports to the European and US markets.

Although there are risks associated with each of the three generic competitive strategies, Porter argues that a firm must pursue one of them. A stuck-in-the-middle strategy is almost certain to make only low profits. A firm in such a position would lack the market share, capital investment and resolve to play the low-cost position, or the focus to create differentiation or a low-cost position in a more limited sphere. To counter this stuck-in-the-middle position, Verdin and Williamson[6] provide a classification of five groupings on which exploitation of Porter's cost and differentiation drivers depend. These are:

1. *Input assets*: e.g. input access, loyalty of suppliers, financial capacity.
2. *Process assets*: e.g. proprietary technology, functional experience, and organisational systems.
3. *Channel assets*: e.g. channel access, distributor loyalty, and pipeline stock.
4. *Customer assets*: e.g. customer loyalty, brand recognition, and installed base.
5. *Market knowledge assets*: accumulated information, and the systems and processes to access new information, on the goals and behaviour of competitors, the reactions of customers, suppliers and competitors to different phases of the business cycle etc.

Explicit recognition of the portfolio of assets that underpins any cost or differentiation driver helps in pinpointing where potential, long-term competitive advantage lies. If all competitors have equal access to the assets necessary to reap the benefits of a driver, then it will cease to be a source of competitive advantage. It is only when it is slow and costly for a rival to gain access to some of the necessary, underlying assets (rendering these assets strategic) that a particular driver will offer scope for sustained competitive advantage. The processes by which the services of particular assets are accessed therefore plays a critical role.

Barriers

Greater competition is associated with more rapid development and the lowering of policy barriers to trade and foreign investment, which is a powerful pro-competitive force. With this in mind, the majority of developing economies (even those classified as G20 nations) are not early entrants into software industry. Some industrialists in the US have advocated government action to limit India's growing position in the software industry. Recent Federal legislation in the US limits competition for work currently being done by government employees to US workers. US Federal regulators may also consider imposing limitations on the sort of work that regulated private sector corporations take offshore.[7] A generic list of examples of initiatives that have been discussed or are actually underway to limit offshore development are:

- limiting national government IT work to signatories of the WTO Government Procurement Agreement or similar such regional agreements;
- bans on government work outside of the procuring country;
- bans on provision of work by non-nationals or holders of visas from specific countries;
- country-of-origin labelling for call centres and Internet-enabled services;
- regulatory bans on work being performed outside of the host country in specific sectors such as financial services and health based on concerns about privacy, security, identity theft, etc.;
- mandatory investigation of individuals offshore handling 'sensitive' information;
- immigration restrictions;
- limiting offshore work to countries with 'open' trading regimes;
- withdrawal of tax incentives for work performed or companies performing work outside of the country.

The issues highlighted above will represent a challenge and strategic focus for years to come. Even with its critical mass, China faces an uphill task competing against established market players such as the US and India. Although China and India face different barriers to entry, it could be argued that to date India has faired better than China and will continue to do so in the foreseeable future.

India, for example, was highly successful in its strategy in outsourcing and generating research and development funds especially for proprietary low-cost product design and technical services. Although the investment and resources required to sell software products globally are high, there are some examples of Chinese and Indian firms accomplishing that goal – but on a limited scale. For example, Sun Wah Linux Ltd (a Hong Kong based software producer) or China.com, that in 2000 was listed on the US based NASDAQ stock exchange where price/earnings ratios tend to be very high.

In order to leverage its position within the software market, the India-based Wipro Group has targeted the IT consultancy, technology, shared services and facilities management markets specifically in the areas of enterprise resource planning (ERP) and customer relationship management (CRM). Wipro's focus for ERP is towards the creation of vertical expertise as well as the pursuit of higher-level alliances with strategic partners. In the CRM sector, their drive is to tap the existing customer base for addition of CRM functionality to their existing ERP. Enterprise application integration (EAI) is another key component of Wipro's solutions portfolio.

Strategic focus: the case for China

The Chinese economy is stronger than ever and, assuming favourable global and market conditions, a low-cost competitive strategy will promote competition and increase efficiency. As a consequence of economic liberalisation, China has been able to take competitive advantage of its low-cost labour and the research and development facilities offered by many Chinese high-technology start-up firms. The availability of China's pool of low-cost skilled researchers and programmers has resulted in a fast and growing presence for multinationals such as Microsoft, Oracle, Adobe, IBM, Lucent, and Intel. Although China has accelerated the introduction of market mechanisms, recent reforms mean that institutional change is uneven and fragmentary, and that the entrepreneurial, managerial and technical skills required for developing globally-competitive firms do remain scarce.

It could be argued that within its own domestic software industry, China has established a low-cost producer base – geared to producing software products well below their market value. A major shift in policy attention to the domestic software industry began five years ago and China's policies to support the software industry have been linked to broader standards and strategy, albeit with the added feature of using government procurement to reinforce this low-cost producer strategy in an effort to compete in bigger markets such as telecommunications, where reforms and market conditions have seen experiential growth.[8] However, if China is to scale up its operations it will need to require some of the creativity and know-how that India has managed to accumulate – some observers would argue that soft and intangible skills such as creativity, technical experience and managerial know-how as well as the capacity for commercialisation are scarce in China. In addition, motivating scarce talent is an issue. The President of KingSoft Co, Bojun Qiu, believes that the greatest challenge in running a software company in China is learning how to motivate and retain talented software developers. Bojun Qiu says '...it is easy for a big international company who adopt some software engineering process to invest a few hundred people to develop one product. We cannot afford that. We often have to ask one person to do what really requires a whole team.'

To enhance its domestic cost leadership position, China has encouraged the development of technological standards.[9] The role of technology standards is assuming growing importance and while it is tempting to attribute China's standards strategy to a narrow techno-nationalism, sensible policy responses to low-cost producer strategies require that the complex motivations behind the strategies be understood, and that China's capabilities and limitations as a setter of standards be recognised. China's market size and increasingly capable technical community give it unique advantages for challenging the established technological architecture found in the international economy[10] In tandem, China is developing more sophisticated software engineering and development capabilities that should contribute to the long-term development of the software industry, and as China continues to attract further FDI (Chapter 1) and grows its pool of top-level computer science and programming talent from its domestic software industry, China could become a formidable technological competitor in the low to medium software markets. Upping ones game, however, requires *skilful execution* in a global economy where established standards already provide a framework for successful economic activities.

According to Suttmeier and Xiangkui[11] *skilful execution* of a technology policy under conditions of globalisation requires steering between the extremes of a narrow techno-nationalism likely to cause friction and resentment from trading partners and a possible marginalisation of one's own industry, and a techno-globalism insensitive to national economic interests. It involves instead moving towards what Atsushi Yamada[12] has termed neo-techno-nationalism, in which one sees both expanded state commitments to technological development (in keeping with techno-nationalist assumptions), but also active public–private partnerships, a more welcoming openness toward foreigners in national technology programs, and greater commitment to international rule-making, policy coordination and economic liberalisation. The notion of neo-techno-nationalism accommodates these changes in ways that the more established ideas of techno-nationalism and techno-globalism do not, as seen in Table 8.1.

The Chinese government's internal networks are complex, and for many foreign firms there are issues that must be negotiated at municipal and provincial as well as central levels. Establishing and maintaining

Table 8.1	The 'isms' compared		
	Techno-nationalism	Techno-globalism	Neo-techno-nationalism
Policy goal: promote whose interest and how?	National interests by preventing globalisation	Global interests by leveraging globalisation	National interests by leveraging globalisation
Who leads innovation (and their respective markets)?	Government targeting	Global market forces	Private initiative and public–private partnerships
Open/closed toward foreigners?	Closed	Open	Open under certain conditions
Prospects for conflict/ co-operation?	Conflict	Cooperation	Cooperation and conflict

Source: Yamada, A. (2000) 'Neo-techno-nationalism: how and why it grows?'.

good government relationships is essential to getting ahead in the Chinese market. Although evidence would suggest that China is increasing its propensity towards market liberalisation, there are of course no absolute guarantees that it will not adopt a techno-nationalism policy. If China places future restrictions and policy measures to primarily focus on domestic software markets, potential consequences may include global isolation, a reduction in high-technology skills, and loss of political and corporate confidence. The techno-nationalism model creates powerful incentives for officials to favour local technology firms in the interest of stimulating growth; while local firms recognise the advantages associated with devoting time and energy to building domestic relationships, they realise this may be a future barrier to globalisation. To improve its future global position China will need to tackle a number of issues. These include:

- its dependence on domestic software markets;
- its access to external high-technology markets (China is perceived to have weak marketing capabilities);
- its access to English-speaking software engineers and other skilled labour;
- its access to external research and development funds;
- its access to the decision makers of multinational firms;
- its access to multinational technology partners;
- its access to high-technology research and development.

In the foreseeable future China, and possibly Vietnam, are likely to be the strongest competition to India. This said, there are clearly overlaps between many of the points listed above. For example, the access to technology markets is premised on having skilled labour, and ongoing access to FDI capital and research and development funds other than local public funding. This will be a big challenge for many Chinese software firms, who are tied to government and other political regimes. Although multinationals in China have not had a significant impact on domestic Chinese software firms, their future role should not be dismissed in that corporations such as Nokia[13] see the positive economic influences on the growth of the telecommunications and related services industries. The strength of Chinese technology policy towards innovation has allowed Chinese firms to compete head to head with the US and other countries on Linux, translation and even security software on their own home ground.

Strategic focus: the case for India

In its 1997 report, the International Labour Office (ILO) praised the emergence of the Indian software industry as a shining example of how third-world countries can take advantage of the liberalisation of trade practices among nations and emerge as world leaders in some industries using their strengths. Since then, the Indian software industry has gone on to serve many sophisticated foreign corporations, many of which are amongst the US premier division Fortune 100 companies. Although India is still reliant on the US for export services,[14] firms pursuing information technology opportunities independently of the US have done well both in terms of profitability and revenue growth. Profitability (profit after tax) of firms such as Tata Consultancy Services has been increasing year on year. Although growth rates amongst Indian firms have been exceptional since 2000, there have been several shakeouts within the Indian software industry that has seen the number of firms drop from 250 to 145, [15] largely due to the redistribution of services and acquisitions within the industry in 2002–2003.[16] In addition, firms that were small could not compete for offshore work. Size and number of years in business determined reputation, and only companies such as TCS, Infosys, and Wipro had a reputation with overseas clients. Most onsite jobs were also linked to offshore jobs. Smaller companies not only did not get offshore jobs, but also consequently lost out on the onsite jobs as well. To raise productivity, leverage FDI and other forms of domestic investment, India has done much to build on:

- its excellent English language skills;
- its ability to conduct business with Western clients in their cultural idiom;
- its established pipeline of customers;
- its internationally-acclaimed reputation of trustworthiness (Indian companies are seen by many multinationals to be transparent and non-discriminate in their business dealings); and
- its reputation for reliability and credibility as a provider of skills and software services.

Although Europe and the United States have both come under fierce criticism for regulating markets, such impending regulations do not seem to have affected India's growth potential. In fact, many new entrants or future software-providing countries such as Vietnam and the Philippines would do well to look first at the incentive features of their investment climate, focusing on those issues that impede competition.

India has been highly successful in targeting its resource base towards a few selected market segments, such as software and managed services, and has benefited in four ways:

1. Through high-technology market knowledge (primary and secondary targeting of multinational firms willing to offload low-value added services).
2. Through lack of direct competition (or English speaking competitors) gaining entry to the market without paying prohibitive entry costs.
3. Through FDI, India was able to create high-technology clusters that leveraged its position in the main software markets.
4. Through the development of long-term relationships – for years Indian firms have been sending their software engineers to work at their European and US clients' sites.

Although India's propensity to undertake outsourcing and software development has served it well, any future expansion must be tied to next-generation markets that are demanding both products and managed services (see Figure 8.2). In order to understand the issues and possibilities of the opportunity matrix, Indian firms will need to consider:

- the creation of products and services that the customers value;
- the market segments it needs to target;
- the expertise within firms to satisfy its target markets;
- the location and spread of distribution channels;
- the criteria for investment (which may include distinctiveness, tangibility accessibility and defensibility);
- future partnerships within the industry, including China (which is strong in product development) both as a competitor and collaborator.

Although India has a significant reputation as a service provider, its maturing technological development capability with expertise in .Net technologies, Java-based components and Microsoft proprietary platforms has provided the foundation for product development. Over the years Indian firms such as Infosys, Satyam, and Wipro have each launched one or more products with varying degrees of market success. Funding any product development strategy is to some degree tied to

| Figure 8.2 | Indian opportunity matrix |

Opportunity Matrix India		
Domestic and International markets	**International markets** Software services, international markets: ■ Large scale software projects ■ Software design and integration ■ Consultancy ■ Full managed services	Software products, international markets: ■ Diversification ■ R&D ■ Joint ventures (China) ■ Digital markets ■ Telecommunications ■ Own R&D IPR
	Domestic markets Software services, domestic markets: ■ Internet services ■ Mobile communications ■ Data services ■ Financial services ■ Education services	Software products, domestic markets: ■ Mobile handsets ■ Open source software ■ Consumer digital products (e.g. low cost iPod) ■ Licensing agreements

future revenue earning. One scenario is to leverage its capability in development and share knowledge with its Chinese competitor: the downside of course is knowledge leakage, in that Chinese firms would take advantage of knowledge gained through collaboration.

Conclusions

Without a doubt, at one level India can see China as a competitor, and at another, a partner. Either way, cooperative situations can turn competitive, and vice versa. In the long-term, if India wants access to the Chinese markets it will have very few options but to partner with Chinese software firms. Although India maintains a strong competitive position over China whether it continues to do so in the future will depend on its capabilities to stay ahead of China's ongoing advances in technology, process and business practice. In the next and final chapter we will explore some of the marketing and customer-oriented strategies used by China and India in its pursuit of global competitive advantage.

Notes

1. Barney (see below) notes that an organisation is said to have a competitive advantage when it implements a value creating strategy not simultaneously

being implemented by any potential competitor (p102). Barney, J.B. (1991) 'Firm resources and substantial competitive advantage', *Journal of Management*, 17: 99–120.

2. Porter, M.E. (1985) *Competitive Advantage: Creating and Sustaining Superior Performance*. New York: Free Press.

3. Ibid, p. 18.

4. CMM model for software engineering is a recognised trade mark (TM) of the Software Engineering Institute (SEI), Carnegie Mellon University.

5. UFSoft has adopted a top-to-bottom strategy: it starts marketing a new product by establishing close relationships with the central government. This makes it easier to sell to local governments.

6. Verdin, P. and Williamson, P. (1994) 'Successful strategy: stargazing or self examination?', *European Management Journal*, 12: 13.

7. WITSA (2004) Global Sourcing Issues paper, February, p. 4.

8. Ministry of Information Industry (2001) 2000 Statistical Report of Telecommunications Development.

9. Standards can lower production and usage costs through economies of scale in production, increase the level of competition by promoting interchangeability, compatibility, and coordination, and lower transaction costs by lowering information and search costs. Standards can also have the effect of increasing the level and efficiency of international trade. Using standards, firms can produce goods with internationally-recognised weight, size, composition, quality, and performance characteristics, or alternatively specify the characteristics of their products based on these dimensions.

10. NBR Special Report (2004) *Executive Summary*. The National Bureau of Asian Research.

11. Suttmeier, R.P. and Xiangkui, Y. (2004) 'China post WTO technology policy: standards, software and the changing nature of techno-nationalism', p. 17.

12. Yamada, A. (2000) 'Neo-techno-nationalism: how and why it grows', *Columbia International Affairs Online* available at *http://www.ciaonet .org/isa/yaa01* (March). See also Ostry, S. and Nelson, R. (1995) *Techno-Nationalism and Techno-Globalism: Conflict and Cooperation*. Washington, DC: The Brookings Institution; and Montresor, S. (2001) 'Techno-globalism, techno-nationalism and technological systems: organizing the evidence', *Technovation*, 21: 399–412.

13. *Computing*, November 17, 2005: 28.

14. The notion of services differs tremendously in that it includes everything from systems integration to information systems solutions and export services.

15. Source Institute of Management India and CMIE data, 2004.

16. The software service (project staffing services) industry was generating extra-normal profit without asking for any investment. This attracted a large number of players at a very fast rate. This resulted in competition and reduced profitability of the firms in this segment.

9

Marketing and customer-oriented strategies

Introduction

The speed of change in the global software industry is quite high, and the global software market chains are increasingly becoming more complex and dynamic. This chapter discusses market- and customer-oriented strategies for the Chinese and Indian software industries in light of the structure and dynamics of the global software industry. Specifically, extending the discussions on competitive position strategies for China and India presented in Chapter 7, this chapter focuses on market- and customer-oriented strategies China and India can pursue to drive their competitiveness in the global software industry. A marketing strategy framework is presented based on which the market- and customer-oriented strategies are discussed for the Chinese and Indian software industries. Following this, implications for the global software industry, other software nations, and consumers of the software industry outputs are briefly discussed.

Marketing strategy framework

Firms can broadly adopt two strategies in approaching markets and positioning their offerings: *market-driven strategies* that require understanding and meeting market and customer needs, and *market-driving strategies* that seek to create new markets and demand for offerings. Figure 9.1 depicts a marketing strategy framework, based on which market- and customer-oriented strategies for Chinese and Indian software industries are discussed below.

Figure 9.1   Marketing strategy framework

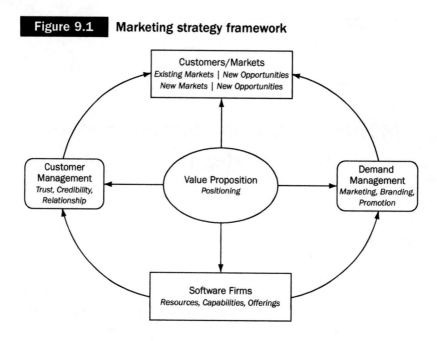

The framework suggests that an effective marketing strategy requires software firms to optimally leverage their resources and capabilities to create offerings that they believe will appeal to their target markets and customers. In order to do so, firms need to possess the requisite resources – financial, physical, and human – as well as scale to match the market opportunities. Software development being a knowledge intensive activity, the availability of high-quality human resources assumes particular importance for a firm's knowledge capability. Similarly, organisational and managerial capabilities and the ability to gainfully deploy the firm's resources are vital for marketplace success. In addition, given the high degree of technological and market uncertainty that characterises the software industry, flexibility to adapt to the changing business environment and customer preferences is an important dimension of a firm's capability.

In order to ascertain market success, software firms need to identify and segment markets in which they wish to operate, analyse the competitive landscape in those markets by performing market intelligence, understand the characteristics of the markets and targeted segments, assess potential market opportunities, and connect their offerings with the targeted market segments through a value proposition that is based on their chosen competitive positioning. The competitive positioning in the value proposition could be lower prices, better quality, better features, better performance, better TCO, or better warranties and support. In order to construct a value proposition that the targeted market segments will find compelling, firms need to understand the customers in the chosen market segments by understanding their businesses, and understanding and anticipating their needs and priorities. Further, firms need to establish credibility with their clients, gain their trust, and develop deep relationships with them.

Finally, and very importantly, firms also need to invest in generating demand for their products and services by actively marketing and advertising their offerings, building and leveraging brands for themselves as well as for their products and services, and by promoting their offerings in their targeted market segments through systematic strategic marketing campaigns and employing other channels such as electronic marketing.

Marketing and customer-oriented strategies for China and India

Based on the marketing strategy framework, this section presents marketing and customer-oriented strategies for the Chinese and Indian software industries structured around the following five categories:

- market positioning strategies;
- demand generation strategies;
- customer management strategies;
- market-influencing strategies;
- partnership leverage strategies.

Market positioning strategies involve designing products and services for identified market segments and configuring a company's response to effectively deal with competition in those market segments. Market positioning strategies embed one or a combination of three competitive strategies, namely cost leadership, differentiation and focus. They also include disruptive strategies that radically change the competitive market dynamic. Superior market positioning strategies focus on value innovation to produce radically superior business value aimed at making competitor offerings irrelevant, expanding the market boundary, and challenging the industry conditions.

Demand generation strategies aim at creating new market opportunities by positioning a company's offerings in such a way that they address their customers' most important problems and priorities and/or help customers realise new possibilities. Examples in the IT industry include transformational programs aimed at life-cycle cost management, enabling superior operational efficiency, streamlining business processes, and improving transactions efficiency. Demand generation strategies focus on developing a compelling value proposition constructed through highly-differentiated offerings for the envisaged markets. Such strategies rely on strategic brand building and leverage, focused marketing (including systematic marketing campaigns), and active promotion in the existing and potential market segments.

Customer management strategies are multi-pronged strategies that include delighting customers through better service quality and superior performance, maximising value deliverance to customers by a deeper understanding of customers' business needs, minimising transaction costs, reducing total cost of ownership, and minimising risks for customers. They also include establishing credibility and trust with customers, developing deep relationships with them and leveraging the relationship capital for driving the customers' business growth. At a more strategic level, customer management strategies include co-opting customers in the definition and delivery of offerings, and partnering with customers in helping transform their businesses and improving their competitiveness.

Market-influencing strategies focus on generating thought leadership with a view to influencing a customers' decision making to the firm's advantage. These strategies include producing white papers and writing influential articles, advertising in print and electronic media, and developing relationships with analysts and the media community, leveraging them to exert influence on the target customer(s) and market segment(s). Lobbying via industry associations and relationships with prominent academics also form part of market-influencing strategies.

Partnership leverage strategies seek to establish business partnerships and alliances with other players in the industry that either provide complementary competencies to compete in the market, or help expand a firm's geographic outreach. Usually such strategies involve pursuit of joint go-to-market arrangements. The complementary competencies and offerings from two partners enhance value to the customers.

Drawing on the SWOT analyses (Chapter 4) and the competitive positioning strategies for China and India discussed in Chapter 7, we discuss the marketing and customer-oriented strategies for the Chinese and Indian software industries, respectively.

Marketing and customer-oriented strategies for the Chinese software industry

The Chinese software industry has developed in response to the domestic market, and it is only recently that it has discovered the lucrative international software services segment. The Chinese software industry has received further impetus due to a growing manufacturing base and presence of MNCs. The development pattern of the Chinese software industry suggests that its competitive scope includes both products and services with an increasing international orientation. However, the main drawback of the Chinese software industry currently is its fragmented structure and overall weak institutional framework that it must correct to realise its ambition of emerging as a dominant software nation. While cost leadership is an inherent advantage the Chinese software industry has, its marketing and customer-oriented strategies must account for current shortcomings. It also needs to build trust and credibility with its international clients, and acquire the capability to deliver large, complex projects remotely. Its marketing and customer-oriented strategy also needs to take into account the fact that its direct rival – the Indian software industry – already has the first-mover advantage in the global software services industry.

For application development and maintenance services, the Chinese firms will need to adopt a cost-leadership based market positioning while simultaneously focusing on demand generation – acquiring customer intimacy by understanding their needs and priorities, and adjusting their service offerings accordingly or creating new service offerings. Initially, Chinese software firms would do well to focus on pursuing many small projects and acquiring experience in dealing with international clients, handling remote delivery, and optimising their delivery model.

In order to deliver predictable and consistent results, Chinese firms will need to achieve higher-quality process maturity and develop robust delivery capabilities. The Chinese software industry could also rapidly diversify itself into the business process outsourcing space, and integrate software services and BPO services from its market positioning. China's location and cultural proximity to Japan, Taiwan, Hong Kong and Korea give it access to a large software services and BPO markets, and in order to benefit from these markets China will need to follow a dual strategy of demand generation and customer management as part of its marketing and customer-oriented strategies.

Achieving scale will have to be an integral part of the marketing and customer-oriented strategies of the Chinese firms for them to gain strength in the services market. Scale will be important for the Chinese domestic services sector as well, because MNCs are increasing their base in China in response to the opportunities in the domestic sector. Market positioning also requires availability of diverse technical skills and English-language proficiency as well as giving confidence to target customers about their business continuity measures.

However, the Chinese software firms will need to quickly strengthen their market positioning strategies by developing credentials in successfully delivering on large, complex projects while owning the entire project management process. Chinese firms will also need to acquire consulting and solution-development capabilities, and this could be done by adopting a partnership leverage strategy. Partnerships with platform vendors such as Microsoft, SAP and Oracle will be a particularly important element of the market positioning to pursue systems integration and package implementation service markets. The large technical talent pool also allows the Chinese software industry to position itself well in the market as a low-cost provider of R&D and engineering services, with proximity to manufacturing being an added bonus.

To operate in the international software services segment, China will need to build up its image and reputation beyond that of a low-cost provider of software services. Therefore, Chinese software firms need to evolve compelling value propositions for their clients as part of their market positioning strategies, with cost leadership as a competitive necessity. Developing trust with clients, establishing good corporate governance, and effectively handling issues pertaining to intellectual property, security and privacy will be required as a key part of the market positioning strategies of Chinese software firms.

Chinese software firms also need to develop strong brands and invest in marketing and promoting themselves beyond governmental efforts in promoting the Chinese software industry. They will need to invest effort in convincing analysts about their market positioning and value proposition, and use market-influencing strategies such as analyst relations to shape the market dynamic. This will be particularly crucial with regard to large outsourcing deals with annuity payments.

The Chinese software industry, however, is in an advantageous position to operate in the products market segment, especially in the domestic and emerging markets context. The phenomenal penetration of the Internet, growing cellular and IP telephony market, boom in the consumer electronics and automotive segments, and a large manufacturing base offers excellent opportunities for Chinese software industry players to develop niche products, including those based on open source software, Likewise, the Chinese software industry has the opportunity to develop products for emerging markets. The marketing and customer-oriented strategies for the product market segment will require adopting cost leadership, alignment with local and emerging market contexts, and radical or disruptive innovations that will sharply differentiate their products from those of competitors and allow rapid market penetration. Chinese software firms could pursue similar international markets by setting up partnerships or joint ventures with overseas firms.

The overall marketing and customer-oriented strategies for the Chinese software industry requires building scale, acquiring credibility in providing end-to-end services, and building a few leading brands. This means that given the cost leadership, the Chinese software firms will need to significantly invest in demand generation, customer management and market-influencing strategies while achieving scale and organisational maturity.

Marketing and customer-oriented strategies for the Indian software industry

The Indian software industry has by and large grown in response to the global market for software and IT services, and Indian software firms continue to pursue opportunities in the software services arena, which is steadily growing. Indian software firms have many years of business relationships with global firms who procure software and IT services from them. However, the Indian software industry now faces growing competition from China, Brazil, Russia, Mexico and some east European countries. Even though none of these countries yet have the capabilities, scale and experiential knowledge required to deliver large, complex projects and serve remote clients, Indian firms must employ ways and means to stay ahead of the pack in order to sustain their leadership position in the global software services and IT services landscape. This means that Indian software firms need to sustain their cost leadership and treat it as a competitive necessity, and focus on maximising value deliverance to their clients by differentiating their services, offering a range of services, and providing different business and engagement models.

For traditional software and IT services such as application development and maintenance, reengineering, application integration and package implementation, the market positioning strategies for Indian firms would include combining cost leadership with differentiation. Indian software firms could deliver differentiation by focusing on helping customers reduce their costs through application portfolio optimisation, aligning their service delivery to customer businesses by leveraging relationship capital, by demonstrating distinct vertical capabilities, and ensuring predictable and consistent deliveries. Focus on other geographies like EMEA and APAC would also be an integral part of the marketing and customer-oriented strategies, as these segments offer enormous growth opportunities for the Indian software industry.

Indian firms can also strengthen their market positioning strategies by rapidly diversifying into other IT services such as infrastructure management, network management, and independent verification and validation services. The global markets for BPO and KPO are huge and Indian software firms could leverage their cost leadership and position themselves in the international market by demonstrating vertical focus, offering productivity gains to customers through operational excellence, reducing customer costs, and by providing integrated services spanning software services, IT services and BPO services. Indian firms could also provide BPO services in other important non-English languages such as Japanese, Latin, Spanish, and German as part of their marketing and customer-oriented strategies, and extend their geographical outreach. However, the Indian firms will need to institute effective measures to deal with security and privacy issues and manage customer perceptions of risk in working with Indian firms.

Indian software firms have economies of scale, provide superior service quality, and have relatively better domain capabilities (when compared to China and others, except large or niche US and European IT consulting and service firms). They also enjoy a good degree of market credibility and a considerable client base. However, in order to sustain their recent double-digit growth, Indian software firms will need to focus on demand generation strategies, proactively understanding target customer problems and priorities and positioning their offerings to address them. This would need to be supported by investment in deploying market-influencing strategies. To accomplish this, Indian firms would need to position themselves in the market as high-end business-IT consultants, and augment that positioning through brand building and targeted promotion, focus on generating thought leadership, and partnering with customers to co-create IT-based solutions to address their business-competitiveness issues. Pursuing joint go-to market strategies with partners could also give a competitive edge to the Indian software firms and strengthen their market positioning.

Indian firms would also need to disrupt the large, total outsourcing deals market, which currently shows a pattern of multi-year, billion dollar deals being awarded to single firms. The Indian firms have an inherent financial limitation in pursuing total outsourcing deals, which often require taking over staff and infrastructure. An effective strategy to compete in such markets would require positioning Indian software firms as specialists in application development and management services, and influencing customer perception that a modular outsourcing strategy would result in better value and less risk for them. Continuous engagements with leading IT industry analysts will need to be an integral part of the overall marketing and customer-oriented strategies for Indian software firms, especially for the international markets, because often the leading analyst firms like Gartner, Forrester and IDC and deal consultants like TPI and neoIT influence market actions and customer decisions.

The ability to effectively deal with issues related to security and privacy will be increasingly crucial for Indian software and IT firms in their ability to provide outsourcing services.

The marketing strategies for the growing R&D and outsourced product-development and engineering services space would need to combine cost leadership, economies of scale, and resource flexibility, and be supported by demand generation strategies aimed at leveraging brands and credibility earned through IT services. The demand generation strategies could focus on emphasising the reduction in fixed R&D and product-development costs, access to a flexible resource pool with skills in diverse technologies, and improved product quality and reduced TCO.

For the domestic services market, the Indian software firms will need to employ similar marketing and customer-oriented strategies as for the international services segment, but perhaps with an enhanced focus on demand generation strategies combined with customer partnering and upstream consulting and advisory services. The marketing and customer-oriented strategies for both the domestic and international SME segments will require market positioning based on cost leadership and hosted services offerings aligned to the characteristics of the SME segment. This will require Indian firms to explicitly communicate their intent to serve the SME segment, promote themselves in targeted SME markets, and tailor their service offerings based on the challenges and needs of the SME sector.

In addition to traditional software and IT services, the domestic market in India offers plenty of nascent opportunities in such areas as e-learning and education services, Internet applications services, and mobile telephony applications. In order to address these opportunities, which have been generated due to a growing penetration of the Internet and cellular telephony, the Indian software industry will need to capitalise on their cost leadership and package a value proposition that is based on a clear differentiation, such as quality of service, on-demand availability, personalisation, security, and/or a distinct feature set. In pursuing these opportunities Indian software firms could adopt partnership leverage strategies, partnering with telecom services providers and Internet service providers. They could also focus on demand generation strategies and work with telcos and ISPs to show how offering value-added services on their networks could give them a competitive edge and expand their business.

The marketing and customer-oriented strategies for the products sector require not only cost leadership and differentiation through better product capability but also distinct market focus and brand building. For example, addressing the marketing opportunities in such areas as application products (e.g. for banking), wireless communication software products, and digital entertainment and media products will require Indian firms to perform structured market intelligence, understand customer needs, establish product-market focus, and differentiate their products in terms of better quality and performance, low TCO, interoperability with other enterprise products, feature richness, and strong security. The positioning for such markets requires strategic marketing based on market segmentation, brand building and active product promotion. Brand building is particularly emphasised for the international segments because Indian firms have traditionally been known for their service excellence, and penetrating the international products market requires not only positioning based on low cost and differentiation but also substantial marketing and brand building.

The marketing and customer-oriented strategies for the lucrative emerging markets such as China and India require low-cost products that are tightly aligned to the emerging market contexts, and the Indian firms could pursue such markets by establishing joint ventures (for example, with a Chinese firm) to gain access to local markets and customer knowledge and by providing support locally.

The IP-licensing opportunities in the semiconductor, media and DSP segments, however, require a market positioning based on cost leadership and a strong value proposition that could include strength of the IP, alignment with the customer's product roadmaps, support and customisation commitments. The software firms pursuing an IP-based business model need to offer flexible royalty models, and invest substantially in marketing and brand building. As the availability of long-term support on the licensed IP is a typical customer concern, the marketing and customer-oriented strategies of firms pursuing IP-licensing business should include customer confidence-instilling measures as part of their business continuity.

China and India – implications for the global software industry

China and India have emerged as two major players in the global software industry, and while India currently has the lead position, China is fast catching up. Over the last three years or so, both China and India have emerged as two major offshore destinations. Their booming economies and emerging markets have received significant attention from global firms and the investor community. With the growing prominence of the Chinese and Indian software industries, it seems likely that these two nations will command a dominating position in the future global software industry landscape. What then are the implications for the global software industry and its customers? Below, we discuss the key implications.

Implications for the global software industry

A competitive scenario analysis of the global software industry suggests that the global product majors such as Microsoft, IBM, Oracle, SAP, Adobe, Symantec, and Computer Associates are likely to continue to dominate the global product markets. These companies face the risk of disruption from the likes of Google or the open source phenomenon, although any mass-scale disruption impacting all product categories is not imminent. Neither it is apparent that the firms in the Chinese or Indian software industry will likely disrupt the established markets for enterprise and mass market software products. However, the local and emerging market contexts in China and India may lead to disruptive software products in niche areas such as communications, healthcare, digital media, and banking applications, which could potentially go on to become leading products in the global markets.

In the software and IT services arena, however, China and India put together are likely to dominate and become barriers to growth for other software nations such as Brazil, Mexico, Russia, the Philippines, and eastern European countries such as Poland and the Czech Republic, assuming China and India are able to sustain their cost leadership. Their dominance will come from the scale of the software industry in China and India. Relative to the other nations, India and China also have first-mover advantage when considered in the context of the global software services industry. In addition, they have both witnessed unprecedented interest from global firms, resulting in a strong business and innovation ecosystem, currently not matched by any other nation. Therefore, unless the software industries in other nations achieve a substantially superior, different, or niche market positioning, it is unlikely that they will ever be in a position to compete head on with China and India.

Implications for customers

Given the vast, low-cost resource base in both China and India, it would be easy to assume that customers would leverage both countries for meeting their business needs. Based on the current maturity of the software industries in China and India, it seems, however, that customers leverage China for low-cost, low-value work whereas they leverage India for high-end capabilities to perform high-value, complex and innovative work. Customers would also divide work between China and India to minimise any risk that may arise from geo-political disturbances in either nation, although evidence suggests that work and investments will be skewed in India's favour owing to its scale, proven capabilities and better institutional framework. Both countries offer attractive emerging market opportunities and here, customers will need to optimise their investments in China and India in such a way as to ensure they get maximum return on their investments. Towards this end, customers may distribute work between China and India to leverage their strengths and complementarities. For example, customers may leverage India's capability in undertaking large scale, complex software development and do the bulk of the product development in India for the global marketplace, locating customisation and localisation work in China to benefit from the low-cost development and proximity to local markets.

Conclusions

As highlighted in Chapter 1, both the Chinese and Indian software industries are growing at a rapid pace and are fast becoming the preferred destinations for software development for the global marketplace. Even though there are other software nations such as Brazil and Russia gaining prominence on the scene, China and India are increasingly acquiring deeper market and customer penetration in the global software industry. Currently, the Indian software industry in particular has a considerable marketplace advantage because of its performance track record, customer entrenchment, attractive cost–value proposition, diverse technical capabilities, industry scale, and managerial abilities, although China is aggressively pursuing the global software markets.

Both China and India enjoy an attractive emerging market opportunity that is set to further fuel the growth of their respective software industries. Economic indicators such as GDP growth, FII and FDI and industry performance metrics such as cumulative aggregate growth rate (CAGR) and manpower strengths point to the growing dominance of India and China in the global software industry.

Index